P9-DGV-475

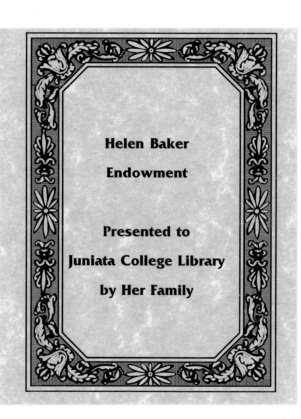

Helen Baker

Endowment

Presented to

Juniata College Library

by Her Family

Charles
Darwin

GIANTS OF SCIENCE

Leonardo da Vinci

Isaac Newton

Sigmund Freud

Marie Curie

Albert Einstein

Charles Darwin

Charles Darwin

By Kathleen Krull

Illustrated by Boris Kulikov

Viking

An Imprint of Penguin Group (USA) Inc.

VIKING

Published by Penguin Group

Penguin Young Readers Group, 345 Hudson Street, New York, New York 10014, U.S.A.

Penguin Group (Canada), 90 Eglinton Avenue East, Suite 700, Toronto, Ontario, Canada M4P 2Y3
(a division of Pearson Penguin Canada Inc.)

Penguin Books Ltd, 80 Strand, London WC2R 0RL, England

Penguin Ireland, 25 St Stephen's Green, Dublin 2, Ireland (a division of Penguin Books Ltd)

Penguin Group (Australia), 250 Camberwell Road, Camberwell, Victoria 3124, Australia
(a division of Pearson Australia Group Pty Ltd)

Penguin Books India Pvt Ltd, 11 Community Centre, Panchsheel Park, New Delhi – 110 017, India

Penguin Group (NZ), Cnr Airborne and Rosedale Roads, Albany, Auckland 1310, New Zealand
(a division of Pearson New Zealand Ltd)

Penguin Books (South Africa) (Pty) Ltd, 24 Sturdee Avenue, Rosebank, Johannesburg 2196, South Africa

Penguin Books Ltd, Registered Offices: 80 Strand, London WC2R 0RL, England

First published in 2010 by Viking, a division of Penguin Young Readers Group

1   3   5   7   9   10   8   6   4   2

Text copyright © Kathleen Krull, 2010
Illustrations copyright © Boris Kulikov, 2010
All rights reserved.

LIBRARY OF CONGRESS CATALOGING-IN-PUBLICATION DATA
Krull, Kathleen.
Giants of science : Charles Darwin / by Kathleen Krull ; illustrated by Boris Kulikov.
p. cm.
ISBN 978-0-670-06335-2 (hardcover)
1. Darwin, Charles, 1809–1882—Juvenile literature. 2. Naturalists—England—Biography—Juvenile literature.
I. Kulikov, Boris, date. II. Title.
QH31.D2K86 2010
576.8'2092—dc22
[B]
2010007315

Printed in U.S.A.   ·   Set in KennerlyH   ·   Book design by Jim Hoover

Without limiting the rights under copyright reserved above, no part of this publication may be
reproduced, stored in or introduced into a retrieval system, or transmitted, in any form or by any means
(electronic, mechanical, photocopying, recording, or otherwise), without the prior written permission of both
the copyright owner and the above publisher of this book. The scanning, uploading, and distribution of this
book via the Internet or via any other means without the permission of the publisher is illegal and punishable
by law. Please purchase only authorized electronic editions, and do not participate in or encourage
electronic piracy of copyrighted materials. Your support of the author's rights is appreciated.

Curr
QH
31
.D2
K86
2010

For science teachers everywhere
                                —K.K.

Charles Darwin

CONTENTS

INTRODUCTION

"If I have seen further [than other people]
it is by standing upon the shoulders of giants."
—Isaac Newton, 1675

CHARLES DARWIN WAS an all-around nice guy.

Everyone liked him—he was modest, agreeable, a sweetheart. A respectable Victorian gent, devoted to his wife and kids. A mild-mannered soul who much preferred puttering in his garden to public speaking. A dutiful son, a loving brother. Kind to his servants. Allergic to conflict. Shy and afflicted with odd ailments, including vomiting so severe that he kept a bowl in his study so as not to disturb the family.

So how did this conventional, pleasant person end up forming what some say is the most influential theory in science, a theory that changed forever how we understand ourselves and the world? How did someone who avoided controversy at all costs become one of the most controversial men in history?

Basically, he couldn't deny what he saw with his own eyes: Darwin was a keen observer of nature, and what he observed in his obsessive studies of wildlife ran counter to the story in the Bible of how all animals, including humans, were created right from the beginning in their final form. Darwin saw that they were continually changing and adapting. Clearly and simply (he's perhaps the only giant of science whose books are read for pleasure), Darwin constructed a theory that explained *how* species change and adapt. His ideas form the basis of all modern biology—the theory of evolution.

Evolution has a particular meaning in biology: it is the process by which all living things change over time, enabling them to better adapt to their environment. Darwin showed how animals and plants evolved over many millions of years from common ancestors.

In centuries past, Galileo and Copernicus had displaced Earth as the center of the universe—and had encountered intense opposition. Darwin extended the scientific revolution they began—he proposed that man was not the centerpiece of creation, separate from and better than all other creatures. No, man was just another species in an ever-evolving world.

Darwin realized he was in for a fight. No wonder we have what is known as "Darwin's Delay," the weird gap in time before he finally published his book *On the Origin of Species*, at age fifty-one. So frightened was he of the backlash to his theory that it took him twenty years to go public with it. Even the process of *writing* his momentous book was long and painful, marked with many bouts of vomiting. Finally, in 1859, gathering all of his courage, he published the book that set out his theory of evolution by natural selection.

His voluminous notebooks make it clear there was no single eureka flash of insight. A self-taught naturalist, he was drawn to all things in nature, from earthworms to earthquakes, stones to spiders, beetles and barnacles to babies. From what he saw, patterns began to emerge and come together into a theory. Darwin always considered his best trait to be perseverance. He was a huge reader, with a hugely open mind. He bombarded scientists all over the world with letters, firing away questions. He had a fierce dedication to getting things right.

Darwin's genius was in connecting dots, which meant he had to see the dots in the first place. A friend said he was "all eyes." Looking more closely and for longer than other people, he literally saw further.

Whose shoulders did Darwin stand on to see so far? First was an early biologist, Carl Linnaeus. In 1735 this Swedish botanist published *Systema Naturae*, in which he categorized the entire natural world. Linnaeus created the system of Latin names we still use— for plants, insects, and animals, and even man: *Homo sapiens*. Linnaeus divided up nature into three kingdoms with main branches for animals, plants, and minerals. From there, he subdivided organisms that were alike into increasingly smaller classifications. Linnaeus mapped the world into a treelike formation, an image that later would become very important to Darwin.

Darwin did not originate the idea of evolution. Before his time, most people believed that species were "fixed," that they had all been created exactly as they were now. But by the early 1800s the idea that species changed over time was in the air, even discussed within his own family. A major cheerleader for it was none other than Darwin's own quirky grandfather. In 1794, Erasmus Darwin published *Zoönomia*, a book in which he clearly proposed that species were not fixed but transmutating or changing. In 1800, Jean-Baptiste Lamarck, biologist and professor of zoology in Paris, began outlining the first complete theory of evolution. France, in fact, claims Lamarck (not Darwin) as the founder of evolution. Lamarck figured out that all current species had gradually developed from a few much simpler ones. But he had no real explanation for how and why this occurred. Because he guessed that all species had a natural drive to improve themselves, Lamarck believed creatures somehow willed changes that would be passed on to their offspring.

A more direct influence on Darwin was Charles Lyell, the eminent English geologist. His theories about continuous changes in the earth encouraged Darwin's ideas about continuous biological change. Thomas Huxley, later to be known as Darwin's Bulldog, wrote that Lyell was "the chief agent in smoothing the road for Darwin."

Then there was Thomas Malthus, an English scholar of political economy. Malthus wrote about the consequences of human population increasing to the point where the number of people exceeds the available food supply. The result? People would have to compete for food, and those who lost the fight would not survive. Darwin saw that he could apply Malthus's ideas to plants and animals.

Darwin's genius idea was the theory of natural selection. Natural selection means that in nature, purely by chance, some members of a species will be born with traits that better enable them to survive long enough to bear young. Over time, after many generations, all members of that species will have inherited these "good" traits. They will have evolved into a new species.

What is a species? Creatures belong to the same species if they can reproduce with each other. Dogs— all breeds—are only one species. But lions and tigers are separate species.

Natural selection showed *how* evolution worked and explained why. Then Darwin supplied, in a way no one else could have, mountains of evidence for his theory.

"I am a complete millionaire in odd and curious little facts," he cheerfully admitted. His interest in nature was unlimited (except for dissection of the human body), and it allowed him to see things more specialized people didn't.

Darwin was lucky.

At the age of twenty-two, he was offered the

chance to sail around the world on the HMS *Beagle*. This voyage to exotic places jump-started his ideas about species.

He was also rich, always financially secure. He never needed a paying job; there was no university he had to answer to, no agenda other than his own, interpreting objectively what he observed. "A scientific man ought to have no wishes, no affections—a mere heart of stone," he said, meaning a scientist had to remain objective, report what the evidence showed, even when the results were controversial.

Darwin lived in the right place at the right time—Queen Victoria of England, who ruled from 1837 to 1901, gave her name to an era of peace and prosperity, allowing for the rise of an educated middle class hungry for knowledge. The theme of this era was progress. It was during Victorian times that "natural philosophers" came to be called "scientists"; science became a profession, not a hobby.

And Darwin was just so nice. Lively and compassionate, he always found people wanting to help him, even as a teenage beetle collector. On the *Beagle*'s marvelous voyage around the world, the entire crew and captain aided Darwin on his collecting missions. Once he published *Origin*, he retreated to his estate, leaving it to friends to publicize and defend his book.

Darwin hated confrontation. Yet he wasn't a wimp. Rather, he said, "I am like a gambler, and love a wild experiment." Indeed, he once wrote, "I cannot bear to be beaten."

Up to the end of his life, Darwin adapted and evolved—and his ideas survived.

CHAPTER ONE
The Dashing Darwin Brothers

WORMS CHURNING SOIL under the lawn, butterflies and bees flitting about the wildflowers, beetles scuttling under logs, birds chirping everyone awake. . . . No wonder Charles Darwin first fell in love with the natural world in the very place he was born.

Nature thrived at The Mount, the Darwin family estate in rural Shrewsbury, England. Born there on February 12, 1809, the fifth of six children, Charles grew up in a large lovely house. It overlooked the river Severn, the longest river in Great Britain. Thanks to its moderate climate, Shrewsbury is called the "Town of

Flowers." As Darwin got older, nearby green fields and dense woods beckoned him to explore.

Shrewsbury is remote. It is one hundred and fifty miles from the teeming mass of humanity called London. With Great Britain poised to become the world's first industrialized nation, factories, new ca-nals, and bridges were springing up all over. But not in Shrewsbury. It remained a sleepy village. At Darwin's birth, so much of what is part of modern existence—electricity, anesthetics, photographs, trains, telegraphs, and telephones—did not yet exist, but all would come during his life.

On both sides, his family was full of accomplished movers and shakers keenly interested in all new devel-opments in science and technology.

Robert, his father, was a larger-than-life doctor—he weighed over three hundred pounds. He treated wealthy patients but made twice as much from his shrewd investments. He donated money to many build-ings in the village, like the town hall, the jail, the infir-mary, the lunatic asylum (as the hospital for the mentally ill was known). Dr. Darwin made a point of attending services at the Anglican church that his patients went to—the Church of England was the official religion of the country, the backbone of England's social order. But in private he and all his family were more freethinking. Some of them—including Dr. Darwin's wife—were even Unitarian, a branch of Christianity that emphasized the importance of reason.

Charles's mother, Susannah, was a more shadowy figure. She was one of the prominent Wedgwoods. Her father was Josiah Wedgwood, immensely wealthy from the pottery company that bore his name. Wedgwood china was used by the royal family and anyone who wanted to be fashionable. Susannah Darwin was well educated, a breeder of fancy pigeons, and a serious gardener. She may have been the first one to explain the parts of plants to young Charles. But she was frequently ill, at the mercy of constant stomach problems.

He was mostly cared for by his three older sisters, whom he called the "sisterhood." His earliest memory was of sitting in his sister Caroline's lap as she peeled an orange for him. The sisters spoiled him but also tried to keep him in line, scolding him for not washing often enough, making sure he knew his Bible.

Charles's other grandfather was Erasmus Darwin, a well-known doctor/poet/inventor/all-around genius. He cofounded the Lunar Society, which met on nights with a full moon. In British scientific circles, it ran a close second place to the all-important Royal Society. These were science clubs for wealthy gents. Josiah Wedgwood was also a member, interested mainly in chemistry that would improve his glazes and clays.

Science was not quite an academic discipline yet, but it was getting there. Still called "natural philosophy," it was considered a fine gentlemanly pursuit along with riding and shooting. (The term "scientist" first appeared in 1834 during Charles's sojourn aboard the *Beagle*.) When Erasmus Darwin wasn't writing flowery verse about the love lives of plants, he wrote an epic medical tract, *Zoönomia*, in which he actually speculated about the idea that species were not fixed, as described in the Bible.

Charles's favorite relative was his gifted brother, also named Erasmus, older by almost five years. They shared all the same interests and genuinely liked each other, Charles struggling to keep up with "Ras" as they dashed along the paths encircling the village.

Charles's first lessons came from Caroline, eight years older, in a room overlooking the gardens. She taught by prodding and criticizing, and he recalled later that he always walked into the schoolroom wondering,

"What will she blame me for now?" At eight he started at the local day school run by the Unitarian preacher.

Charles enjoyed inventing secret codes. He also made up elaborate stories "for the pure pleasure of attracting attention and surprise." He played hoaxes, claiming to see rare birds when he hadn't, and once tricking a friend at school into believing that he could make flowers bloom in different colors by watering them with specially colored water. He craved admiration, though he outgrew the need to lie.

Everyone remembered him as quiet, easy to get along with, a boy who avoided conflict. He had a mild stammer and, for several years, a special problem pronouncing words starting with "w." He could often be found underneath the dining room table, reading *Robinson Crusoe* and other favorites. He was a big reader, following the lead of his idol, Ras, who recommended books and encouraged his taste in literature.

One day his father gave him two treasures—illustrated books from his personal library. One was on insects, the other on stones and minerals. Charles found his father, who was an imposing, sometimes stern man, a bit scary, but also called him "the kindest man I ever knew." Wandering among the orange trees, flowers with glorious scents, and vegetable beds, Dr. Darwin shared his interests with Charles. Sometimes he took his son out in his yellow carriage on his rounds to patients—a tight squeeze for Charles next to his bulky father.

His happy world broke apart when frail Susannah died as Charles was turning eight. In later years he said he had hardly any memory of his mother. He himself called this memory lapse "odd," as have many historians, unless it was the first example of his later flair for banishing a painful subject from his mind.

Dr. Darwin never remarried and continued to run his family as a tight ship, becoming even more overbearing.

It was around this time that Charles developed what he called "a passion for collecting." Collecting was a popular gentlemanly pursuit, but he went all out, with bugs and worms, especially beetles, live and dead; as well as shells, birds' eggs, butterflies, pebbles and minerals, and more. At age nine his goal was to know something about every single stone on the path to the front door. A few years later, he took up bird watching with vigor. In fact, a friend once said he was "all eyes," and Ras teased him about "those telescopes you call

eyes." (Darwin himself thought he was all nose—he was self-conscious about it until the end of his life.)

At nine, he was sent away to the private boys' boarding school in the center of town, where Ras had been going for the past three years. Shrewsbury Grammar School was a little over a mile away, fifteen minutes from The Mount, but it was another world.

The school trained rich boys to enter a university like Cambridge or Oxford. The older boys carried loaded guns and sometimes threatened each other, the food was terrible, beatings were frequent, the blankets on Charles's bed were always damp, and for years afterward he could summon up the memory of the stench of some thirty chamber pots underneath the boys' beds.

At Shrewsbury, only the classics were taught—Greek and Latin, ancient history and geography. There were no science classes. The beliefs of the Church of England lay behind everything that was taught in school, so everyone would have taken for granted the Bible's description of the origin of the world. It was created in six days and populated with all the animals looking then the same way they still did in current times. The creation of Adam and Eve was the pinnacle of God's work.

Charles was not a good student. Once the headmaster even yelled at him and humiliated him in front of the whole school for wasting his time. But for almost seven years, he was stuck at Shrewsbury School. "Nothing could have been worse for the development of my mind."

He desperately wanted to be outside, lifting up stones to discover insects, inspecting the surface of a pond, exploring with Ras. He actually ran away from school whenever he could—dashing home after attendance was taken, racing back for nighttime lockdown. If he'd been caught he would have been expelled. That would have made his father very angry.

When Ras took up chemistry, Charles did too. A revolution was taking place in chemistry. One of the pioneers was Joseph Priestley, who, about thirty years earlier, had been one of the discoverers of oxygen, and had published a history of electricity. The Darwin brothers knew all about Priestley—their own uncle Josiah Wedgwood had helped to fund Priestley's research, partly for business reasons, since Wedgwood was looking for advances in glazes and clays.

The brothers took over a toolshed in the back garden. This was their official "laboratory" for performing simple experiments as outlined in their copy of William Henry's *Elements of Experimental Chemistry*. They analyzed minerals, coins, crystals in various stones and minerals, tea leaves, and the effects of the sun's rays on various things, using household items like sewing needles to create simple tools.

Equipment was a problem. They started off with a thermometer, fireproof china (courtesy of Uncle Josiah), and a lamp that supplied the flame for heating gases and chemicals. They had vast plans for more, but their penny-pinching father kept them on a tight leash. Arguing with Dr. Darwin was generally pointless. Whenever the brothers did get money from him, they called it "milking the Cow," and spent hours debating what to buy, drooling in shops that sold test tubes, minerals, blow pipes.

Their favorite occupation was to set off explosions. But they were also ambitious, trying to duplicate the experiments of Robert Boyle, one of the founders of modern chemistry, the author of *The Sceptical Chymist.* They hoped to isolate a new element, like Humphry Davy, who several years earlier had discovered sodium and potassium and helped identify the elemental nature of chlorine and iodine.

They did succeed in manufacturing nitrous oxide, or laughing gas, first discovered by Priestley. Taking laughing gas was a craze at the time. Charles's nickname became "Gas." He also did experiments on the gaslights at school, until the headmaster found out and gave him a lecture, complete with a pull on his ears.

Dr. Darwin had decreed that both of his sons were to follow him into medicine. It was a blow when Ras departed for Cambridge University, leaving Charles behind. For three long, lonely years, Charles struggled on at Shrewsbury School on his own.

Every weekend he rushed home to work in the lab. The two brothers exchanged long letters, Ras offering advice about the lab from a distance. "If the Cow is not utterly consumed at the next milking," he suggested, "it would be a very good thing to buy as many of the large green, stoppered bottles as possible."

By 1825, Ras was about to graduate from Cambridge. Now he would continue his medical studies with a year of practical work. Dr. Darwin couldn't help notice that his younger son was not doing at all well at Shrewsbury. He decided to pull sixteen-year-old Charles out of school ahead of time and send the pair of them to Edinburgh University in Scotland.

The Darwin brothers—together again—were off to become doctors.

CHAPTER TWO
Sickened by Blood

ODDLY ENOUGH, NO degree was required for practicing medicine in Darwin's day. In fact, Charles, like Ras before him, spent his sixteenth summer as a sort of junior doctor, helping his father treat the poor of Shrewsbury. He had up to a dozen patients of his own, mostly women and children not sick enough for the hospital. He'd note symptoms for his father to identify, then would make up the prescriptions himself. Some potions were iffy at best—a baby with a cough might be given a mixture of opium, sherry, and brown sugar—and harmful at worst.

Dr. Darwin was convinced that Charles had the

makings of a brilliant doctor. He thought his son had a talent for "exciting confidence" in patients, which he believed was the key to medical success. His son was much less sure about his future in medicine, but one seldom questioned Dr. Darwin.

Now Charles was at Edinburgh University, a hub of science, to study medicine and follow in the wake of his brother, father, and grandfather. It was exciting to be in big, bustling Edinburgh. The first year he hung out exclusively with Ras, attending some of the same lectures, eating meals with him. Ras set a record for borrowing more library books than any other student, and Charles was close behind. He also bought a copy of A *Naturalist's Companion* by George Graves, to use along the Scottish seaside. The brothers went for regular Sunday nature walks to fishing villages on the Firth of Forth, examining tide pools, looking for interesting shells and stones, buying oysters covered with tiny creatures to dissect.

But as for medical school—not much to like. At Edinburgh, the professors' income depended on how many students signed up for their courses, which meant that classes were like popularity contests. Teachers competed and feuded with each other in unscholarly ways. Classes were noisy free-for-alls, with students stamping their feet to show agreement, hooting their disapproval, using trumpets and peashooters when particularly irked.

Darwin was highly critical of most of his professors. One was "so very learned that his wisdom has left no room for his sense." Of another he wrote, "I dislike him and his Lectures so much that I cannot speak with decency about them." The classes themselves—anatomy, surgery, midwifery, chemistry, materia medica (today's pharmacology), and natural history—he either found "intolerably dull" or dismissed as "useless."

Visits to the operating theater traumatized him. Patients screamed in agony as amputations and other procedures were performed without anesthetic. The most upsetting was when the patient was a child—witnessing such operations "haunted" him for years. For the rest of his life, the sight of blood made him severely sick to his stomach.

He unenthusiastically passed his courses, but it was a lot more satisfying to be outside in the fresh air, collecting, riding. Also, he took up shooting with a vengeance, so eager that he kept his special hunting boots by his bedside, ready to go at a moment's notice.

In an odd (for someone who loved nature) but utterly fashionable way, he was an avid hunter—rabbits, rats, pigeons, partridges, pheasants—killing as many as three animals a day.

He did spend time at Edinburgh University's natural history museum, one of the best in Europe. He made friends with John Edmonstone, a freed black slave who mounted specimens there. Edmonstone was someone Darwin greatly admired, and from him he took private lessons in taxidermy, the art of preserving and stuffing dead animals.

He also liked his chemistry teacher, the popular Thomas Charles Hope. The brothers had outgrown the lab, which had turned back into a toolshed. But chemistry still intrigued them, and they both fell for Hope's showmanship. Hope attracted classes as large as five hundred for his highly visual lectures, conducting experiments with equipment so expensive he did not allow students to touch it. So the class was all talk, no hands-on experimentation.

After a year of medical school, the most important thing seventeen-year-old Darwin had learned was this: he did not want to be a doctor. He was interested in everything in nature *except* the human body. To avoid an argument, he kept this news from his father. Another reason for his silence was money: he now had a clearer understanding about just how rich his father was. Darwin realized he would probably never have to work for a living, much less practice medicine, if he didn't want to. So there was no reason to make waves.

Thus he dutifully returned to Edinburgh for his second year, without Ras, who was off to attend a school of anatomy in London.

This year Charles avoided corpses and blood as much as possible. He missed Ras, but he started hanging out with other students, got new calling cards, and became very fashionable. Darwin even started to take snuff (smokeless tobacco sniffed through the nose). He joined the Plinian Natural History Society, named for Pliny the Elder, an ancient Roman with vast interests, who had written a famous natural history of Rome. It was a science club—favoring botany, geology, zoology—that met in an underground room to read and discuss papers. The club had been founded by Robert Jameson, a noted professor of geology, a few years earlier.

Jameson had translated the works of French biologist Georges Cuvier, who came up with the important new theory of Catastrophism: at one point, long ago, Cuvier believed, the earth had undergone a series of violent geologic changes. These catastrophic events explained why the earth had different layers of rocks and why certain species had died out.

In his introduction to the translation of Cuvier's work, Jameson wrote that the biblical flood could be counted among these world-changing catastrophes. This statement made the Church very happy. As for Darwin, he found Jameson stiflingly boring (he called him "that old brown dry stick"), but he did learn something about geology from him.

Robert Grant, a thirty-three-year-old lecturer in zoology, took Darwin under his wing. For some four months he worked with Grant in marine zoology. Grant taught him how, with the help of a microscope, to dissect marine life—simple creatures like sea worms, sea slugs, mollusks. The unusually open-minded naturalist began taking Darwin as his guest to lectures and meetings not open to undergraduates. Grant shared his latest ideas with Darwin, thrilled to be conversing with the grandson of the famous Erasmus Darwin.

One day Grant dropped his guard and praised Jean-Baptiste Lamarck's views. Lamarck was a French biologist, a professor of zoology, who had proposed an early theory of evolution, which he called transmutation. He suggested that life had started with a few simple species that changed and developed over time into the vast array of complex animals and plants of the modern world. Lamarck believed that nature was on the move, not static. However, he mistakenly believed species could will these changes to happen and pass them along to future generations.

Someone, either Grant or Jameson, had published an anonymous paper in 1826 praising "Mr. Lamarck" for explaining how the higher animals had "evolved" from the "simplest worms." It was the first use of the word "evolved" in the sense we use it today. Darwin was probably the first person with whom Grant shared his thoughts on evolution. Not until he was an established professor would Grant come forth publicly.

Darwin had already encountered these ideas in his grandfather Erasmus's *Zoönomia*. Erasmus proposed that one of the scientific laws that governed the natural world was transmutation by acquired characteristics. "Would it be too bold to imagine, that . . . perhaps millions of ages before the commencement of the history of mankind, all warm-blooded animals have . . . arisen from one living filament?" he wrote. Life possesses "the faculty of continuing to improve by its own inherent activity, and of delivering down those improvements by generation to its posterity, world without end!" Erasmus believed the "first great cause" created that "living filament." By "first great cause" he meant God.

Thanks to his work with Grant, Darwin made his first Plinian presentation with his own discovery: the black particles found in oyster shells were the eggs of a skate leech, not seaweed spores, as previously thought. Then he went on to discuss something else he'd discovered under his microscope: what he first thought were eggs were actually larvae. Why? Because they were moving by themselves, something eggs can't do. Darwin had seen under his microscope that what he had thought were the spores of a type of seaweed called *Flustra* seemed to be able to move by themselves. This had never been observed before. He had rushed to tell Grant—this was Darwin's first taste of the thrill of scientific discovery.

But Grant's reaction was not at all what Darwin had expected. Grant was miffed; he felt Darwin was treading on his territory. He warned Darwin not to publish his findings. Darwin was heartsick and embarrassed.

Never enthusiastic about his future career in medicine, Darwin—with help from the sisterhood—tried to convince his father to let him quit. Dr. Darwin was furious. "You care for nothing but shooting, dogs and rat-catching," he yelled, "and you will be a disgrace to yourself and all your family."

He remembered this humiliating scolding, word for word, until his death. It was probably the low point in Charles Darwin's life.

CHAPTER THREE
A Beetle in His Mouth

THE EVER-PRACTICAL Dr. Darwin came up with a Plan B. If Charles couldn't be a doctor, then he could be a clergyman in the Church of England, a country Anglican parson.

As usual, Charles didn't argue. He agreed with his father that it was wrong to be merely "an idle sporting man." He had to have some profession, and this was a respectable one that would allow enough free time to continue studying nature. Most naturalists at the time were clergymen in the tradition of Gilbert White, who viewed exploring the "wonders of God's creation" as part of a minister's duties. Charles had some concerns about the requirement to declare a belief in *all* the dog-mas of the Church of England, but he still believed in the truth of everything in the Bible.

So at age eighteen, Darwin went off to Cambridge University to study theology. Former classmates of Ras's helped Charles get settled. He was jazzed to live in rooms that the theologian William Paley had once lived in. Darwin admired Paley's *Natural Theology*, which took as proof of God's existence the complexity of living beings. Nature's design could be used to prove the existence of God. Charles wrote, "I do not think I hardly ever admired a book more than Paley's *Natural Theology*: I could almost formerly have said it by heart."

He later said that these years at Cambridge were his happiest. His schedule was undemanding, allowing time for foxhunting, pigeon shoots, fishing, exploring the countryside around Cambridge. In the evenings he drank claret and played blackjack, freely spending Dr. Darwin's money. He joined the Glutton Club, which met for dinners of "birds and beasts which were before unknown to human palate." The members feasted on hawks, herons—though they disbanded after the owl dinner. His interests included music—he couldn't carry a tune but greatly enjoyed attending concerts. He also

began going to museums and studying art books, an-other way of learning how to see.

In his cousin William Darwin Fox, who was older by four years, Darwin found a kindred spirit, almost a second Ras. Fox was on the same career path as Charles, and like him also much happier outdoors than in. Both of their rooms overflowed with stuffed birds, baby chicks, various specimens.

The competitive collecting of beetles was a na-tional craze, and Darwin became crazed. He hunted for them, tearing bark off dead logs, scooping through swamp gunk, burying a snake and digging it up weeks later to check for insects. Then he'd put his finds in a tin box until he could get back and pin them. He spent hours mounting and cataloguing his collection. He even hired assistants to bring him bags of moss scraped off old trees in the hope of finding more rare specimens. Once a friend sketched Darwin riding a beetle, with the caption "Go it Charlie!"

On one memorable day, ripping off some old bark, he found two rare beetles and grabbed one in each hand: "Then I saw a third and new kind, which I could not bear to lose, so that I popped one into my mouth. Alas . . ."

The third beetle spewed out a terrible-tasting fluid that burned Charles's tongue so badly, he spit out the beetle. Two out of the three beetles escaped.

With better results, he sent his beetle records to the entomologist James Francis Stephens. To Darwin's delight, Stephens published about thirty of these records in *Illustrations of British Entomology*. This marked the first appearance of Darwin's name in print as an author.

He found a first love in one of his neighbors, Fanny Owen, though her letters revealed she knew perfectly well she was competing with beetles for his attention.

He began spending a lot of time with John Henslow, a professor who was making botany the most exciting subject at Cambridge. Charles had already heard from Ras about this fascinating teacher. Author of *A Catalog of British Plants*, Henslow lectured on the chemical properties of plant tissues, plants that could be used in medicine, how plants adapted to different environments, how they were fertilized. His classes included hands-on dissection of plants—so much nicer than cutting into humans, Darwin thought.

"What a fellow that Darwin is for asking questions!" said Henslow, who began inviting him to a weekly open house for heady chats with professors and serious students. In general, the Cambridge atmosphere stifled independent thought—it was even stuffier and more orthodox than Edinburgh. But a few professors, like Henslow, were liberal thinkers. Yes, God's laws were the ultimate authority, but conventional theology and science could coexist. These progressive thinkers were shifting from a literal interpretation of the Bible to a metaphorical one. In this light, studying nature was seen as studying God's work, with no conflict between science and religion. Science was not the enemy of religion; falsehood was the enemy of both

Thirteen years older than Darwin, Henslow became a father figure: "He is quite the most perfect man I ever met with," Darwin said of him. He ate his meals with Henslow's family and went for many long walks with him. He used Henslow's microscope to study the structure of cells in orchids and geraniums. In contrast to Darwin's old teacher Robert Grant, Henslow rejoiced in whatever discoveries Darwin made, and was kind when pointing out which of his "discoveries" weren't actually new.

To remain teacher's pet, Darwin sometimes would go to foolish lengths. One day Henslow led students on a field trip to hunt for bladderwort plants. They were given poles in case they encountered muddy ditches and needed to vault themselves across. Darwin spotted a perfect specimen, but when he tried to vault across to get it, his pole got stuck in the straight-up position. Undeterred, he slid down the pole and into the muck, got his specimen, and proudly if sloppily carried it over to his laughing professor.

Henslow's influence was both academic and personal. He once wrote to Charles about his tendency to be oversensitive: "One of your foibles is to take offence at rudeness of manners and of any thing bordering upon ungentlemanlike behavior, and I have observed such conduct often wounds your feelings far more deeply than you ought to allow it."

He also spurred Darwin to read John Herschel's new *Preliminary Discourse on the Study of Natural Philosophy*. Herschel believed that nature was governed by laws, and that the highest aim of natural philosophy was to discover these laws through an orderly process of active induction balancing observation and theorizing. The scientific method, as it would come to be called.

Henslow probably also got him to read Alexander von Humboldt's sensational *Personal Narrative of a Journey to the Equinoctial Regions of the New Continent*, about his five-year journey to the Canary Islands and around South America. Humboldt and Hershel sparked in Darwin "a burning zeal to add even the most humble contribution to the noble structure of Natural Science." He drifted into fantasies about making discoveries in exotic locations. Writing to his sister Caroline, he said, "My enthusiasm is so great that I cannot hardly sit still on my chair. . . . I have written myself into a Tropical glow."

Hiring tutors, he crammed for exams and passed his courses with relatively high marks (tenth out of 178 students who didn't go on for advanced or honors classes).

Darwin's plan for the summer of 1831 was to join classmates to study in the tropics—at Tenerife, the largest of the Canary Islands, said by Humboldt to be a paradise for naturalists. The trip fell through. In July Darwin went to book passage and found that passenger ships to the Canaries departed only in June.

Meanwhile, Henslow introduced Darwin to his old tutor, the great Cambridge professor of geology Adam Sedgwick. Darwin had diligently avoided Sedgwick's classes, still disillusioned by the boring geology classes

classes, still disillusioned by the boring geology classes he'd taken at Edinburgh.

But now Henslow asked Sedgwick to take Darwin as his assistant on a geological walking trip through Wales. Darwin overcame his resistance to geology and agreed. Before the trip he even practiced using his "clinometer," the tool for measuring mountains, on the furniture in his bedroom.

As The Mount was on the way to Wales, Sedgwick offered to meet Darwin there. That night Darwin, all excited, told the professor a story he'd heard of a tropical shell found in a nearby gravel pit. This news contradicted the known geology of the area. Sedgwick gently pointed out Darwin's naïveté. The shell could have landed there in a number of ways that had nothing to do with the geological makeup of the land. Just one shell was not nearly enough evidence to overturn established knowledge.

From this, Darwin learned "that science consists in grouping facts so that general laws or conclusions may be drawn from them." It was better not to draw conclusions without lots of proof.

Sedgwick's goal in Wales was to correct errors in earlier geological maps of the area. These maps, which recorded different types of rock layers (strata), were used by scientists to learn the geological history of an area. Darwin quickly learned how to identify rock specimens, interpret rock strata, and generalize from his observations. Sometimes he went off on his own, and he and Sedgwick would meet up later and compare notes. When Sedgwick made use of some of Darwin's findings, it made Darwin "exceedingly proud."

He returned to The Mount with a new passion for geology. He vaguely looked forward to Cambridge in the fall and continuing his studies to enter the church. Ras, whose delicate health had forced him to give up medicine and live off his inheritance, was more cynical and made fun of Charles's lack of proper religious fervor. With two weeks to kill before school, Charles went off for some intense shooting with his Uncle Josiah.

On his return home, there was a letter from Professor Henslow. Henslow had been asked to recommend someone—a gentleman—to work as an unpaid naturalist aboard the HMS *Beagle*. This ship of the Royal Navy was going to explore the coast of South America and its ports. Ensuring the safety of trade routes was a crucial step in expanding the mighty British Empire.

After that the *Beagle* would continue on to the South Sea Islands and Australia, circling the world over the course of two years. If new gold or diamond deposits were located, so much the better.

The ship was sailing from Plymouth in a month. Would Darwin be interested?

Silly question.

CHAPTER FOUR
The Journey of a Lifetime

A TRIP AROUND the world . . . seeing birds, bugs, and flowers he (and most naturalists) had never seen before . . . on a ship with a library of 250 books, including the latest science books and the complete *Encyclopedia Britannica* . . . out of school, away from his nagging father, treated with respect as the ship's naturalist. . . .

To the twenty-two-year-old Darwin, it all sounded incredibly exciting. He had no real idea what he was letting himself in for, but it seemed like a fantastic opportunity, for what he didn't know yet. "I immediately said I would go," Darwin wrote later.

But first he had to get around his father's serious objection to the "wild scheme." The risks were too high—harsh conditions, disease, shipwreck, death—and the whole idea meant yet another delay in Charles's settling down to a proper profession. Darwin went to Uncle Josiah for help. Point by point, Josiah answered the objections of Charles's father, and the doctor finally changed his mind.

The captain of the *Beagle* was twenty-six-year-old Robert FitzRoy. It was an English custom to take a naturalist along on such trips for information gathering. Basically, FitzRoy was looking for a nice guy, someone easy to be around, a cultured gentleman he could talk to as an equal at meals. The previous captain of the *Beagle*, overwhelmed by responsibilities and with no real peer to talk to, had shot himself. Intensely ambitious, conscientious about every detail, FitzRoy wanted to avoid conditions that could lead to this fate. He was interested in science himself, especially astronomy and meteorology, and had bought six of the ship's twenty-two chronometers (for determining longitude) with his own money.

The two men met and liked each other, though the captain worried about Darwin's nose. A believer in the pseudoscience of phrenology—analyzing personality

from a person's features and the bumps on his skull—
he didn't think Darwin's nose showed enough stamina
to withstand the rigors of this voyage. Still, traveling
with the grandson of Erasmus Darwin sounded very
cool. Darwin was able to persuade him that his "nose
had spoken falsely."

So the deal was on. Darwin promptly set about
meeting with London naturalists for advice on what
and how to collect, spending quality time with Ras,
advising the sisterhood on packing up his things and
labeling his shirts with his name. "I am as happy as
a king," he wrote. Besides materials for collecting and
preserving specimens, a portable dissecting microscope,
and other high-tech gadgets, he packed a Bible, John
Milton's epic religious poem *Paradise Lost*, his own copy
of Humboldt's *Personal Narrative* (a gift from Henslow),
and *Principles of Geology*, volume one, by lawyer-turned-
geologist Charles Lyell (a gift from FitzRoy).

Alas, FitzRoy's meticulous preparations, then several winter storms, delayed the trip for several months.
Discouraged, Darwin spent his time in Plymouth, fear-
ing he'd made a big mistake. He developed a rash on
his face and pains in his chest, but he refused to visit a
doctor for fear of being told he couldn't go.

Finally, on December 27, 1831, the voyage got off

to a sickening start. This was not a cruise ship. Darwin had a tiny cabin under the poop deck, which he shared with two roommates, a fourteen-year-old midshipman and a nineteen-year-old survey officer. To sleep in his hammock each night he had to pull a drawer out of the wall so his feet could tuck in. Darwin was seasick beyond belief. He spent the first several days vomiting nonstop, eating only raisins. The misery was "far far beyond what I ever guessed at."

And then there was the harsh treatment of the crew. With seventy-four men under his command, mostly younger than he was, FitzRoy was paranoid about establishing discipline immediately. He ordered twenty-five to forty-five lashes given to any sailor guilty of drunkenness, disobeying orders, or neglecting his duties. Darwin was horrified by the cruelty and the nightmarish screams of men being whipped. He felt like he was in hell. His distress was obvious to FitzRoy, who assumed Darwin would be leaving the ship at the first port.

But soon enough, he was being soothed by nature—the brightly colored fish jumping around the bow of the ship, the warm breezes, a storm of butter-flies. He began lowering gauze nets, thrilled at the intri-

cate sea creatures—the plankton and jellyfish—he was
catching. These tiny, simple forms of life never ceased
to amaze him—"that so much beauty should be appar-
ently created for such little purpose."

He started keeping a journal for the first time, training himself in the discipline of putting his thoughts into
words on paper, developing his powers of observation,
learning how to write in a clear, unpretentious style.
In three weeks the ship reached St. Jago in the Cape
Verde Islands, 450 miles off the African coast. Darwin

eagerly rushed ashore to investigate. The dense green jungle, with its palm trees, orange trees, coffee plants, strange new bugs, rich colors of the valleys, unfamiliar birds—he was in heaven. "It has been for me a glorious day, like giving to a blind man eyes," he wrote. After tasting bananas for the first time, he set about harvesting every specimen he could find, exclaiming out loud with pleasure.

Throughout the voyage, he never lost his enthusiasm for anything new. He was like a kid in a candy store: "If the eye attempts to follow the flight of a gaudy butterfly, it is arrested by some strange tree or fruit; if watching an insect one forgets it in the stranger flower it is crawling over." He collected tiny insects, reptiles, fish, birds, mice, corals, barnacles, dried bulbs and seeds of plants, rock specimens, shells, and, of course, beetles.

At one point, Darwin described his mind as "a perfect *hurricane* of delight and astonishment." In a rock pool, he marveled at a cuttlefish changing color as it hurried for cover. He succeeded in catching another and taking it back to the ship, where it put on a show by glowing in the dark. Charles was amazed, thrilled, transported by this discovery. Only later was he told that these were typical, well-known cuttlefish talents.

Aboard ship, he was too seasick to read much. He was only halfway through Lyell's *Principles of Geology*, but he was very impressed. Lyell, like Leonardo da Vinci centuries before him, reasoned that Earth's mountains and valleys had formed over enormously long periods of time. The Earth must be at least hundreds of millions of years old, not a few thousand as stated in the Bible. Lyell saw that "the present is the key to the past," meaning that the same forces acting on Earth now—such as volcanoes, earthquakes, floods—have always been the cause of change on the planet. Over time lots of small events led to big changes.

This was new news, opposed to what Darwin's professors had taught about Cuvier and isolated catastrophic events.

Trying to reconcile Cuvier and Lyell—they couldn't both be right—kept Darwin's brain busy. He happily "geologized" his way through the trip, starting in St. Jago, the site of an ancient volcano. Exploring a streak of white rock that turned out to be compacted coral and seashells, he noticed that the embedded shells were the same as the live sea creatures on the beach. So this layer must once have been a seabed, underwater. The level of the white streak varied, but there were no dramatic breaks in the white streak, so it didn't seem to have arisen from a sudden catastrophe. The land must have risen from the ocean gradually, as the result of a long series of volcanic events over many years.

Landing in present-day Salvador in Brazil, Darwin was delighted by the tropical forest but disgusted by slavery, banned in Britain but still legal in other countries, including the United States. Darwin's family was strongly abolitionist, so he was shocked to find that Captain FitzRoy was pro-slavery, believing it was part of the natural order of things. Uncharacteristically, Darwin was drawn into a huge argument with him about it. Afterward FitzRoy apologized, then they never spoke of it again.

As for his attitude toward native people he encountered over the course of the voyage, Darwin attributed differences between people to cultural advantages, to "civilization" (British, of course, being the best), not racial inferiority. Humans around the word were ultimately and "essentially the same creature," he wrote, but their societies were at different stages of development. Today Darwin's views seem elitist and condescending, but for the time his thinking was progressive.

By 1832 Darwin was in the Brazilian rainforest, delighting in butterflies, parrots, and army ants. After

seeing a group of vibrantly colored flatworms undulat-
ing in the shade, he started his flatworm collection,
marshalling some fifteen species.

When they were onboard ship, he and FitzRoy
settled into a routine. After breakfast in the captain's
quarters, they went their separate ways. Darwin would
tag his specimens, record every observation, make duplicate copies of his lists to be on the safe side, keep
up his journal, and write long letters back home. The
two men took lunch and dinner together, enjoying each
other's company, discussing the novels of Jane Austen
and the glories of that day's scenery. Darwin did notice
that the captain had a temper (the crew's nickname for
him was "Hot Coffee"). For the most part FitzRoy treated Darwin affectionately, as a sort of mascot. One of
FitzRoy's tasks was to name places, and Darwin Sound
in Tierra del Fuego and Mount Darwin in the Andes
were showing up on his maps. Very religious, FitzRoy
would lead long services every Sunday, which everyone onboard was required to attend.

Seasickness continued to plague Darwin just about
every time the ship sailed—"I hate every wave of the
ocean with a fervor," he wrote. To get relief he would
lie down on the table he was supposed to be working
on. "I must take the horizontal," he would plead.

But whenever they hit shore, he regained his stamina. He was always first to disembark, and then would work at full speed to collect. With no guarantee he'd ever be returning to any locale, he worked like a demon to maximize his time. He arranged with FitzRoy to stay longer on land whenever he could.

Floating around Bahia Blanca Bay, he noticed fossils embedded in the banks. On the spot, he dug up what he could. The next day he returned to dig up the head of a bizarrely big animal. Not until several hours after dark was he able to get the beast's head on board. It was later identified as an extinct giant sloth Megatherium, one of the largest animals ever to walk the earth. Farther on, he found more fossilized Megatherium bones, as well as bones from another extinct creature, one that resembled a gigantic armadillo. These fossils were among his most amazing discoveries. They interested Darwin because the extinct creatures seemed to be giant versions of animals currently living on Earth. Were they related? If so, how? Had the extinct creatures "transmutated" into animals the nineteenth century world knew?

In the 1830s little was known about fossils. The first fossil bones to be identified as coming from large extinct reptiles had only been found in 1822. Scientists now understood that long ago certain creatures had lived on Earth and then disappeared. But what accounted for their disappearance remained a mystery. Some attributed their extinction to the flood in the time of Noah.

By now Darwin's collections of specimens sometimes threatened to take over the ship. With every single one, he asked questions: Why was it like this? How did this shape or form develop?

His mind was wide open, and this was his real education. "I owe to the voyage the first real training or education of my mind," he wrote. He had the luxury of all this time to contemplate, without pressure to publish or conform to some professor's teachings. And since Dr. Darwin was paying for all Charles's mounting expenses, Darwin owned his collections, everything he found. It became important to him to retain control, as he planned to donate his collection to the best and most central museum he could find in England.

Whenever he reached a port city, he shipped boxes of specimens back to Henslow for real experts to analyze. He also picked up his mail, often finding books he'd asked Ras to send. Late in 1832, pulling into Buenos Aires, Argentina, he was glad to receive his copy of volume two of Lyell's *Principles of Geology*.

In Patagonia, he reported the massacre of native Patagonians by the Chilean army: "Every one here is fully convinced that this is the most just war, because it is against barbarians. Who would believe in this age that such atrocities could be committed in a Christian, civilized country?"

He was more carefree in 1833, while riding the Pampas plains with Argentinean gauchos. From the cowboys, as they hunted and fished, he learned of their creation stories. Trying to be suave in throwing his bolas around as the cowboys did, he once tripped up his own horse, and everyone roared.

Still an eager hunter, Darwin contributed to the ship's food supply with deer, guinea pigs, tuna, sharks, and turtles. One year, he personally supplied all the food for Christmas lunch. On occasion he accidentally ate valuable specimens. Once, in the middle of a meal, it occurred to him that he might be consuming a new species of ostrichlike bird, something he'd actually been looking for. He was able to save parts of it (a species that's known as Darwin's Rhea).

Darwin hired one of the crew as his assistant, but all the men were interested in Darwin's work and often helped him or kept him company. FitzRoy pointed out that Darwin "makes everyone his friend." The crew brought some of his best specimens and made useful introductions for him at ports of call; to those who didn't know what a naturalist was, they would explain that Darwin was "a man who knows everything." They called him Philos, short for ship's philosopher.

It wasn't all fun. There were storms, and once the ship hit a wave two hundred feet high. On land, there were hairy escapes from bandits as well as nights spent sleeping on the ground, attacked by gigantic bugs. In one house he woke up with bloody spots on his shirt, his body entirely covered in flea bites.

Aside from seasickness, Darwin actually fell ill only once during the trip, in 1834, but he was bed-ridden for six weeks. What caused him to be so sick remained a mystery . . . possibly sour wine, possibly South American sleeping sickness from a bug bite, possibly acute food poisoning made worse by toxic medicines. During this low point of the trip, he wrote, "Our voyage sounded much more delightful in the instructions, than it really is." He even made plans to quit and go home. At the same time, FitzRoy's moodiness increased from the burden of his duties, and he had to be talked out of resigning.

Both men snapped out of depression after witnessing nature at its most dramatic. In southern Chile, while they were safely onboard ship, a volcano erupted right before them. They stayed up most of the night using a telescope to observe giant chunks of fiery lava spewing forth.

Then, exploring the forest in Valdivia, Chile, Darwin experienced his first earthquake. The land he stood upon shook for a full two minutes, a shock to someone who till now had always experienced the earth as solid and firm under his feet. Thirteen days later in Concepción, he saw the immense damage caused by the quake—the town in ruins, a hundred people dead. Nature wasn't just a romp. But what most attracted his attention was that the land near shore had risen almost eight feet. Mussels that had once thrived underwater were now clinging to exposed rocks way above the surface of the waves, dying in the sun.

Firsthand, he was witnessing a shift in the earth's surface. It was happening right then, in his own time. With Cuvier and Lyell still arguing inside his head, Darwin was leaning toward Lyell: land was constantly changing, rising and falling.

Riding into the Andes Mountains, he saw beyond the spectacular scenery—wondering "who can avoid admiring the wonderful force which has upheaved these mountains, & even more so the countless ages which it must have required."

He was still vaguely assuming this voyage was all one big detour and he'd be entering the church back in England. But nearly four years had passed, and all his separate ideas were piling up, ready to coalesce and explode.

CHAPTER FIVE
Galápagos

*T*HE TRIP THAT originally was to take two years stretched into five.

Luckily for Darwin's stomach, a good part of the time was spent on land, a total of three years and one month. While FitzRoy mapped shoreline nooks and crannies or had the ship repaired, Darwin traveled inland, sometimes farther inland than any European had before.

Four years into the voyage, in 1835, the *Beagle* reached the wild, isolated Galápagos Islands. Darwin could not know it at the time, but this stop was to be the defining moment of the trip, the defining moment

of his life as a scientist. Six hundred miles west of Ec-
uador, the islands were collectively named in Spanish
for the giant tortoises lumbering about. Though now
famously associated with Darwin, the islands were
little known at the time, mainly the destination of pi-
rates hunting turtles for meals and prisoners bound for
a small penal colony.

The Galápagos, an archipelago of twenty or so islands in sight of one another, were created from the
eruption of underwater volcanoes. The black, rocky
land, formed from lava, almost appeared to be in various
stages of decomposition. To Darwin it seemed as if he
had set foot on an alien planet with powerful wind and
ocean currents streaming in from every direction. The
islands were home to an astonishing array of creatures
that lived nowhere else, as well as plants unknown to
the western world.

Darwin was in heaven. Penguins and sea lions living alongside flamingoes, flying fish, male frigate birds
inflating their throats to look like red balloons, stunning tropical birds like the red- and blue-footed boo-
bies, yellow warblers—all with no fear, so tame they
would come right up to him. The tortoises truly were
giants, measuring seven feet around. Black marine

iguanas, the only sea-going lizards on Earth, lolled, almost camouflaged on the craggy black rocks, so "disgusting, clumsy" that they made him laugh out loud. Yellowish land iguanas, with a "singularly stupid appearance," were "torpid monsters."

Today, Darwin's treatment of the wildlife would be considered boorish at best, criminal at worst. There was no such concept as "endangered species." He felt entitled, as a scientist, to poke and probe. He threw stones at the birds to test their reactions and pushed a hawk out of a tree with his gun. Over and over, he threw a marine iguana into the sea, proving only that it really didn't like to be in the water. He pulled another iguana's tail until it looked right at him as if outraged. He lifted up a tortoise's shell to see how much it weighed—it hissed at him in response. He rode another one like a horse, rapping on the shell to get it going.

One night Darwin was invited to dinner by the British governor in charge of the penal colony on one of the islands. Just making conversation, the officer said something odd. He mentioned that he could tell by the shape of a tortoise's shell which island it had come from. At the time Darwin didn't think much about this, but later when he looked over his notes, his brain went

into overdrive. These islands were cut off from each other—there was no interbreeding among tortoises. So was the particular environment of each island responsible for changes in the species?

Eventually he pondered the enormous ramifications of this in his journal: "If there is the slightest foundation for these remarks the zoology of Archipelagoes will be well worth examining, for such facts (would) undermine the stability of Species." In other words, species might not be permanent; they could change.

This journal note could have been called his breakthrough, his eureka moment, but as of then it was just a sense. He had nothing to back it up, and he had learned how important it was to have evidence. He wasn't going to figure all this out until much later. But—his mind was starting to race with possibilities.

He was in the Galápagos for a month, and he was happy to leave. The islands were stark and creepy. The temperature was always boiling hot. After capturing eighteen tortoises for upcoming meals, the crew of the *Beagle* set sail. Everyone onboard was looking forward to the next stop—the balmy paradise of Tahiti in the South Seas.

It took another year before the *Beagle* returned to England. After New Zealand and Australia, it was on to the Cocos Islands, seven coral islands off the coast of Perth. Here Darwin had a chance to investigate the reefs of living coral, wading up to his waist in warm water that teemed with tiny bright fish. He started to wonder just how coral reefs were formed, gleaning evidence to be sorted out later.

The ship sailed around the tip of Africa, detoured once more to the east coast of South America for more mapping, and finally headed back to England.

Darwin had written almost 1,400 pages of notes on geology, almost 400 on zoology, and a diary of 770 pages. He'd amassed well over 5,000 specimens, many already shipped home, some dried, some preserved in alcohol, some still alive. He was returning skinnier but full of ideas.

One decision he made on the way home was that killing animals for sport was wrong. He vowed to give up hunting.

Desperately homesick, exhausted with the new, he set foot on British soil on October 2, 1836. "Oh, the degree to which I long to be once again living quietly with not one single novel object near me!"

He was a changed man. The trip had developed his powers of observation and appreciation for the wonders of nature. He had seen things few people had, with enough material for several books. He saw clearly now his purpose in life. He was not meant for the Church. Being a naturalist in his off hours was not enough. He wanted to be like Lyell. He would give his life to science—contributing to the world's knowledge was utterly honorable in itself.

He also realized that he was done with travel. Ras had bought a house on Great Marlborough Street in London, living the leisurely life of a socialite. Darwin wrote to ask him to look for a nearby place for him to live.

Back on British soil after four years, nine months, and three days, he knew he'd had the experience of a lifetime. He never left Great Britain again, and for the next forty years, barely left his house.

CHAPTER SIX
Um, Now What?

*A*T TWENTY-SEVEN, Darwin had evolved, matured, grown up. Even his father could see the change, exclaiming when he first saw him: "Why, the shape of his head is quite altered!"

Darwin returned something of a celebrity, at least in science circles. His name had a buzz. For that he owed Henslow. While Darwin was gone, his old professor had unpacked shipments of specimens that Darwin kept sending ahead. He had to rent a room to store them—the spiders, butterflies, shells, birds, glow-worms, bearded monkeys, green parrots, and beetles.

Along with a whole rainforest in miniature, Darwin had sent letters trying out his new ideas. Acting like an unpaid promoter, Henslow had done his former student the enormous favor of getting his samples into the right hands and reading his letters to the right people.

Also, the giant Megatherium head had been exhibited in London and caused a sensation. Vestiges of extinct animals were the rage.

In some ways he was a stranger in a strange land. At eighteen, Princess Victoria was about to become Queen Victoria and begin her sixty-four-year reign. For the rich there were indoor bathrooms, gaslights, lawn-mowers, new steam technology, railroad tracks criss-crossing the country, more factories, more shops, more books and magazines. In *Oliver Twist* Charles Dickens was to reveal the miseries of the poor, the thousands of orphaned children working in factories or living on the streets of crowded, polluted London.

Soon Darwin moved, with two pet tortoises, to London, just down the street from Ras. After their separation, the two brothers were closer than ever, dashing around town to visit Ras's many friends. Darwin tried to understand Charles Babbage, inventor of the earliest computer, and with even less success, the early feminist Harriet Martineau.

Darwin's top priority was to catalog the specimens from his journey. He kept some for himself and distributed the rest among experts he admired. They would identify them and bestow official Latin names.

Among the specimens were many birds from the Galápagos. Darwin had not marked from which specific island the different birds came, because he hadn't thought it mattered, since the islands were so close. A famous ornithologist named John Gould studied the birds and came to a startling—to Darwin—conclusion.

To the ornithologist, all the Galápagos birds did look closely related. But that did not mean they were one species. After all, horses and donkeys look quite similar and can even mate, yet they still remain separate species. (Their offspring, mules, cannot reproduce.) The differences that Gould discovered among the finches meant they had to belong to separate species—thirteen *different* species of finches.

The most important difference was the shape of their beaks. For instance, some had beaks that were short and good at cracking open seeds; some had much longer beaks that were good for picking bugs out of bark.

Darwin now realized that each bird's appearance

must result from the environment of its native island.
Some islands were covered in trees whose bark was
bug-infested. Other islands were covered in plants that
produced seeds. Not recording the finches' place of origin had certainly been a mistake. But Darwin still was
able to recover enough information on their origin to
form a brilliant theory.

Perhaps a single species of finch had flown from
the mainland of South America to different islands of
the Galápagos. Over time, depending on the environment of the island on which it landed, this single species adapted in different ways that helped it survive on
its specific island. The finches on the different islands
changed to the point where they became separate species. This was a huge piece of the puzzle, but Darwin
had yet to identify the way it happened . . . that was to
come later.

Much to his pleasure, he met his hero the geologist Charles Lyell, and even better, became good friends
with him. Lyell took him around to all the important
men of science, like John Herschel, who wrote that the
"mystery of mysteries" in science was how species were
"replaced" by others. Most important for Darwin's career, he became a close friend of botanist Joseph Hooker,
on whom he bestowed all his plant specimens.

A bit embarrassed by all the attention, Darwin buried himself in work. While groaning that "writing is the
most tedious and difficult work," he spent his first nine
months home polishing his *Beagle* journal. (It came out
two years later as volume three of FitzRoy's account of
the *Beagle's* two voyages.) He had ideas for several more
books—on zoology, geology, coral reefs. . . .

He also began keeping a series of small notebooks
with him at all times so he could jot down his own
thoughts or interesting points others made. Full of
misspellings and cross-outs, lacking punctuation, the
notebooks were a way of talking to himself. These
notebooks include what are now called the Transmutation Notebooks, his first, baby-step attempts to unite
his observations that would pave the way to the development of a theory.

Eventually, Darwin filled fifteen of these notebooks, which were labeled alphabetically. The A
notebook was devoted to questions about geology. He
called the B notebook "Zoonomia," in homage to his
grandfather Erasmus. In it Darwin made a now-famous
drawing of a simple tree. It was 1837.

He was a terrible artist and had done no sketch-
ing during the voyage of the *Beagle*, but this tree didn't
have to be fancy. Branching out from its trunk were

species—modern species at the top, their ancestors at the bottom. It was a Tree of Life, representing how all animals and plants could have descended from a common ancestor. Some simple form of life changed and branched off into more complicated organisms. Above it he wrote the words, "I think."

In the B notebook, Darwin also speculated, for the first time in his writings, that species survived or died out depending on their ability to *adapt* to their environment.

The C notebook was mostly about heredity, the passing down of traits from one generation to the next. At one point he wrote that once you accepted the possibility that one species might change into another, then the "whole fabric totters and falls!" By fabric he meant the traditional idea of unchanging life on Earth, including the biblical story of Genesis in which all species were created from the very first in their final form. Was man the exception to what he was pondering? No, he didn't see why man should be excluded from the tree. Man was just another species, part of nature. Knocking human beings off their pedestal, Darwin knew, was not about to go over well. So before going public, Darwin set about finding evidence.

He began visiting zoos, parks, and farms, obsessively interviewing gardeners and animal breeders, gleaning facts about how they purposely sought to improve a particular species. Crossbreeding was a huge craze in Great Britain, with people trying to develop better strains of pigs, flowers, potatoes, whatever. Breeding experts were always happy to talk about methods they used to produce improvements in a species.

Now came an "aha" moment. Darwin realized that over time reproduction could lead not only to improvements within a species but to the beginning of an entirely new species. This process happened all by itself in nature, with nothing controlling it. Random forces! No one in control! It's easy to understand how frightening this worldview would have been to Victorians.

Darwin was also reading everything he could get his hands on. The dramatic rise of printed matter in England gave him much to choose from, and he made long lists of books, checking each one off as he finished it.

In 1838 he encountered the Reverend Thomas Malthus's *Essay on the Principle of Population*, first published forty years earlier. This influential clergyman and English scholar wrote about evil—and why it exists in the world. He also talked about the problems of

an industrial society, such as overpopulation. A minister, he believed that God created famines. They would
keep human population in check, and their purpose
was to inspire mankind to strive to improve his situ-
ation. Malthus drew parallels to nature. He observed
that plants and animals will always produce far more
offspring than can survive, given a limited food supply.
The weakest will not survive long. The stronger, more
able, more industrious individuals will have a better
chance of surviving and having offspring.

The struggle for existence—Malthus viewed it in
terms of people and society. But what hit a chord with
Darwin was the idea of a competitive environment in
nature. He immediately drew a line from Malthus's argument to the "warring of the species," the struggle for
existence among plants and wildlife.

Whoa.

As he wrote later, "Here, then, I had at last got a
theory by which to work." For Darwin, reading Malthus was the closest thing he had to a eureka moment.
Things started clicking into place. Species were always
reproducing beyond the resources available to them.
Which individuals would survive, and which wouldn't?
And why?

Darwin applied what he learned from Malthus to what he already knew about crossbreeding plants and animals. He now printed up a questionnaire about crossbreeding and sent it to everyone he could think of. How did they choose which individuals in a species to breed? What methods did they use for selective breeding?

Darwin took a long view of the information he received. In nature, purely by chance, were new species created? He began seeing patterns in adaptation. For example, in a litter of rabbits some might be born with longer legs. Assuming that long legs were useful to survival, those rabbits would be the ones to live long enough to mate, and some of their children would inherit their longer legs. Over time, in generation after generation of litters, the long-legged rabbits would be dominant. Short-legged rabbits would die out. Might a new species eventually arise that were like rabbits but with longer legs? Could this pattern hold true for all species? Was this how new species formed?

Into the D notebook, he wrote about glowworms, cattle, ducks, and Malthus. "There must be some law that whatever organization an animal has, it tends to multiply and IMPROVE on it," Darwin concluded.

And he wrote about Darwins. He interviewed Dr. Darwin about unfamiliar branches of the family tree, looking for traits and stories, adding to those he already knew.

By E he was referring to "my theory"—through natural selection a species changed over time and developed into a new species.

Darwin paid several visits to the London Zoo to observe an orangutan, Jenny. Jenny and another recent arrival, a chimpanzee, were among the first members of the ape family that the English had ever seen. Viewers were somewhat shocked to watch Jenny interact with her keeper in ways familiar to anyone who knows a small child. Queen Victoria said later she found Jenny "painfully and disagreeably human."

On one visit Darwin observed Jenny's reactions while he played a harmonica and gave her peppermints to eat and leaves from a lemon verbena plant to smell. To him her behavior as she pouted and whined to get what she wanted was *exactly* like "a naughty child." Into a notebook he scribbled, "Man from monkey?"

The notebooks had many more questions than answers.

By notebook N he was writing that biology followed natural laws that could be tested and proven, as laws in physics and astronomy were. "We can al-

low satellites, planets, suns, universe, nay whole sys-
tems of universe, to be governed by laws," he pointed
out, "but the smallest insect, we wish to be created at
once by special act." By "special act" he was referring
to God's creation of a fixed world. He knew the general
public wasn't ready to accept his ideas. He had to keep
his notebooks secret, even from Ras and his new best
friend, Lyell. Though he didn't take the precautionary
step of writing backward, as Leonardo da Vinci had in
his notebooks three hundred years earlier, Darwin had
similar motives for keeping his ideas to himself.

Darwin started to have trouble digesting his
nightly roast beef. But that didn't stop him from thinking about his theory, and then thinking about it more.
Up until now he had been flailing amid facts; now they
were forming patterns. Branching out from alphabeti-
cal notebooks, he started writing an essay on the free
paper at the posh Athenaeum Club, to which he'd been
elected a member at the same time as Charles Dickens.

He lost another eighteen pounds. He was plagued
with stomach pains, vomiting, severe boils, heart pal-
pitations, trembling. The drugs that doctors gave him,
like opium, probably made him worse.

This was the beginning of the long period later
known as "Darwin's Delay," the years in which he

avoided publishing the book about his theory. The delay lasted twenty years. Various factors contributed—he was a master at procrastination; he had a great deal to fear by going public, so he wanted to amass tons of irrefutable examples to prove his theory; and besides, he was busy.

All of this dwelling on reproduction within a species as the driving force of nature merged with something more personal—his own thoughts of marrying.

His former girlfriend Fanny had married someone else almost as soon as he left on the *Beagle*.

Would a wife add to or detract from his life?

He was torn. Ras had never married and seemed happy. It wasn't as if he needed someone to act as a hostess—Ras did that for him, planning dinner parties in his honor. And his time was completely his own.

Darwin listed the pros and cons of marriage on paper, as if assessing and describing a new kind of beetle. "A nice soft wife on a sofa with good fire" versus giving up traveling to America, going up in a balloon, the "terrible loss of time" away from his studies.

But adventuring had lost its appeal. At age twenty-nine, he was a bachelor who lived in his armchair, whose main hobby was keeping track of his own ailments.

CHAPTER SEVEN
"Confessing a Murder"

*T*HE URGE TO mate won out. And he didn't look far for someone to mate with. After calling on her a few times, Darwin chose to marry his first cousin, thirty-year-old Emma Wedgwood, daughter of Uncle Josiah, and a friend since childhood. After the proposal, she felt "bewildered" and he had a headache. But her answer was yes.

Darwin didn't want an intimidating wife. Emma, however, was well educated for a woman of her day, could speak four languages, and had even studied piano with the famous composer Frédéric Chopin. Emma was exceedingly pleasant, a natural born caretaker. "I think you will humanize me," he wrote her, "and soon teach me there is greater happiness than building theories and accumulating facts in silence and solitude."

Plus the union kept both their fortunes in the family. Prone to nightmares about being penniless, Darwin felt safe knowing that, if he had a future family to support, Emma's money meant his lifestyle would never have to change. He could still put all the time he wanted into his studies.

As for Emma, she called him "the most open, transparent man I ever saw . . . sweet-tempered." A nice guy. So nice that she could blot out their differences concerning religious faith. Against his father's advice, he confessed to her his doubts that the Bible's version of the history of the earth could be taken literally. Emma, a devout Unitarian, calmly decided that while she regretted the "painful void" between them, she could agree to disagree, in a sort of don't-ask-don't-tell way.

After a small wedding in January 1839 at a church near her country estate, they shared sandwiches and a bottle of water on the train to London.

That same year, Darwin's journal, popularly known as *The Voyage of the Beagle*, was published. (It appeared first as one volume in FitzRoy's account and was so popular that it was then published separately.) In his book, Darwin speculated about those Galápagos finches: "Seeing this gradation and diversity of structure in one small, intimately related group of birds, one might really fancy that from an original paucity of birds in this archipelago, one species had been taken and modified for different ends."

Captain FitzRoy never liked the book—since the voyage he had become even more religious, and he was appalled at Darwin's science. The two men were becoming increasingly estranged.

But as a well-written and spellbinding travel book, the *Voyage* was hugely popular with everyone else and is still read for pleasure today.

Darwin was working hard, not terribly focused, distracted by his own reproductive success. While living in London, he and Emma had two children, William Erasmus and Anne Elizabeth. He viewed them like a scientist would—a very fond scientist. William was his "little animalcule of a son." He started drafting a natural history of babies, with detailed notes on his son's first year. Every little thing about his children fascinated him—the first smile, blinking, what their tears meant, the acquisition of language, how they reacted when tickled or when Darwin sneezed loudly, when they were naughty (he wrote about it rather than punishing them), how they perfected "the art of screaming" because it was "of service" to them, how they lived in joy and pleasure.

At thirty-three, Darwin needed to move his growing family. He and Emma looked at the new railroad lines to make sure they picked a place close enough to London to make the round trip regularly. Ras would always keep a bedroom for him on Marlborough Street, but for the rest of his life, Darwin would live at Down House, a country estate in the village of Downe, near Bromley, some sixteen miles outside London.

For Darwin, Down House, on its eighteen acres of wooded land, was a return to the haven of nature that The Mount in Shrewsbury had been for him. It was remote, with trees and flowers of all kinds, the loud humming of bees, the blackbirds singing. (Twenty years previously, the fossil of a giant lizard had been found only thirty miles from the house, and just that year the word "dinosaur" had been coined to describe such creatures.)

His first change was to lower the road along the house and plant bushes for privacy. In his study, behind a curtain in the corner, was a nook where he could throw up in private. He positioned a mirror outside the window so he could see visitors coming and flee, and also so he could see the mailman coming. Taking full advantage of the superb British postal system, which delivered mail to his neighborhood as many as four times a day, he sought information from all over the world. He wrote letters, lots of letters, to other naturalists, asking nicely, in flowery language, for help. Some 14,000 letters to and from him survive; more have been lost.

Eventually the Darwins had ten children, although in an era of high child mortality, only seven survived to adulthood. Victorian fathers were supposed to be remote and stern, but to the surprise of just about everyone, Darwin was a dad who enjoyed children. He kissed them, bathed them, tickled them, danced them on his knee while singing, stroked their hair as he walked by, listened intently to their concerns. They were allowed the run of the house for romping and games, and they loved hanging out in his study, with its jars of worms, beetles, and spiders. He used pictures in his science books to entertain them. He would tell them stories or let them write their stories on the backs of old paper. They could run in for art supplies

or whatever they needed—except when they needed
bandages for cut fingers. These they would get when
he went out for a walk, because they knew how much
blood upset him.

The light of his life was his daughter Annie. With
pure joy at living, she wrinkled her nose when laughing,
was musical and loved dancing, and would play with his
hair for half an hour, making it "beautiful." Like him
she was very neat—she loved looking up words in dic-
tionaries, identifying colors, sewing little things for her
collections of dolls. To him she radiated happiness and

"animal spirits." He thought ahead to how much she would cheer him and Emma up in old age.

Sometimes Annie danced ahead of him on the daily walks taken with his fox terrier, Polly. Thinking endlessly, he took a path called the Sandwalk along a woods, cut off from the sight of any building, just forest and valleys. He would pile stones at the turn of the path and knock one off at each turn. Five turns meant he'd walked his quota of half a mile. The children could hear the click of his walking stick and the stones being knocked off.

In this way, the years passed.

Baby steps became longer strides. In 1842, in between writing up his *Beagle* zoology and geology projects, Darwin wrote the first draft of his evolutionary theory, his working hypothesis, thirty-five pages, not for publication. He was starting to use the term "a natural means of selection"—natural as opposed to man-managed breeding practices.

"At last gleams of light have come," he wrote in 1844 in a famous letter to his friend Joseph Hooker, "and I am almost convinced (quite contrary to opinion I started with) that species are not (it is like confessing a murder) immutable. . . . I think I have found out (here's a presumption!) the simple way by which species become exquisitely adapted to various ends."

"Like confessing a murder"—so great was his dread of going public. He also feared upsetting Emma. Her biggest concern was always that his religious doubts might separate them in the afterlife. She wrote him an eloquent letter about this that he read over and over, writing at the bottom that he had kissed it and cried over it.

But it was to Emma that he gave the second draft of this essay. He revised and expanded his original essay into 230 pages in 1844, showed it to no one, and wrote Emma in detail as to how she should have it published in the event of his death. With his customary modesty, he wrote: "I have just finished my sketch of my species theory. If, as I believe . . . my theory is true, and if it be accepted even by one competent judge, it will be a considerable step in science." He put the letter and es-say into a brown folder and stuck it on a shelf.

It was a case of drastic avoidance.

Then a bombshell struck. A book called *Vestiges of the Natural History of Creation* was published anon-ymously that same year. Like Darwin, the author be-lieved that all forms of life had descended from a few much simpler beings. He even went so far as to suggest that the ape might be man's ancestor. The author used many of the same sources as Darwin, such as Lyell, and had some similar ideas, but one of his conclusions was quite different—he thought God had provided a plan that nature followed as it evolved. The author never revealed himself publicly, but he was Robert Chambers, a Scottish journalist. Born with twelve fingers and twelve toes, he had a deep interest in abnormalities, which in turn prompted him to theorize about how humans were created.

The book provoked an uproar. Most scientists looked down on it as the work of a "dabbler." Darwin's old professor Sedgwick trashed it as being so crazy it must have been written by a woman. Still, it played to a huge new interest in popular science and was a blockbuster that every smart person—including Florence Nightingale and Abraham Lincoln—was reading.

Glued to a copy at the British Museum Library, Darwin thought "Mr. Vestiges" made many mistakes and was too bold in his leaps. His research was slipshod, all secondhand—he hadn't traveled much and thus had no firsthand observation or evidence to back up his ideas. It was all speculation.

The book gave Darwin a shock—other naturalists were forming ideas about the development of new species. Still, that didn't mean he was ready to take the giant step of publishing his own book.

He thought vaguely about moving his family to "the middle states of North America"—the terrain sounded exotic to him. Instead, for the next fifteen years, he hardly left home, gathering as many facts as humanly possible that would buttress his theory. Delaying, delaying, delaying.

CHAPTER EIGHT
Yet More Delay

FOR EIGHT YEARS Darwin threw himself into what seems like an odd scientific detour from his species book. He turned his microscope and dissecting tools to . . . barnacles, those humble sea creatures found clinging to rocks or the bottoms of boats. They may not sound exciting, but as he found out, "Truly the schemes and wonders of nature are illimitable." It was already known that barnacles were hermaphrodites—both male and female. But Darwin was finding all kinds of strange forms, like a male with two sexual organs, males that appeared to live inside of females—forms that seemed to show intermediate stages between male and female.

A family tragedy interrupted his work. In 1849, all three of his daughters got scarlet fever, and his beloved Annie never regained her health. She died in 1851 at the age of ten, probably from tuberculosis. Emma and Charles were devastated. He tried to console himself by writing a ten-page memorial to her, about all the qualities he had treasured, most of all the way "she held herself upright, and often threw her head a little backwards, as if she defied the world in her joyousness." The sadness of her early death haunted him for the rest of his days.

In eight—yes, eight—years of work on barnacles, looking at and dissecting some 10,000 specimens, Darwin was able to show that slightly changed body parts served different functions to meet new conditions. He sensed some of his friends were laughing at him. But the work did fit in with his species book, after all. The variations in barnacles showed what evolution could look like, that nothing was constant, that all species have come from simpler forms that were both male and female. And in 1853 the first of his four volumes on barnacles earned him the Royal Society's Royal Medal. This formally established his reputation as a biologist, beefing up his credentials for publishing what was to come.

Darwin claimed he lost two of his barnacle years to illness—boils, insomnia, a "swimming head," what we today might call panic attacks. Stomach problems were common, even fashionable, among Victorian intellectuals. But Darwin's stomach took the prize—throbbing worse than ever, with spells of vomiting and extreme flatulence that lasted for weeks.

Historians still debate what was ailing him. The arsenic he used to preserve specimens may have poisoned him, or perhaps the huge doses of a toxic laxative prescribed by doctors were to blame. It could have been some baffling disease inherited from his mother, who died so young. He could have picked up a parasite from his trip around the world. His seasickness could have been mysteriously and permanently reactivated, with a vengeance. Did he have allergies or lactose intolerance? Was he a serious hypochondriac? He probably wasn't helped by all the coffee he drank and snuff he took.

If he had been a woman he might have been diagnosed as a hysteric. A man acutely sensitive to criticism, Darwin knew his theory was in for a ton of it. Perhaps his worries about his species book were manifesting themselves as physical symptoms. Or perhaps the symptoms were a useful way to avoid social life and concentrate on his work. Or a way to get Emma's full attention, since she was always quick to set aside other duties to nurse her husband through any bout of sickness.

Darwin had access to the best doctors, went for second opinions, also third, fourth, and fifth. He tried every known remedy, including quack treatments. The only thing that seemed to help temporarily was going away to a spa and taking the newly fashionable water cure. On the doubtful theory that cold water drew blood away from the stomach, treatment involved torturous stuff like freezing showers and being wrapped up mummy-like in cold wet sheets. He was supposed to take fresh air, limit his work to two hours a day (but he found ways to cheat), and stick to a bland diet that included bananas but not the figs and dates he loved.

On one spa visit he felt so good that he went for thirty days without nausea. The treatment induced "the most complete stagnation of mind: I have ceased to think even of Barnacles!" Outside his house, he installed a cold shower, and the children could hear him groaning in there, coming out on cold days almost blue.

With the barnacle work finally over, he continued to develop his theory of evolution through reading, consultation with other naturalists, and observation and experimentation in his garden and in the country-side around Down House. By now his house was like the *Beagle*, with Darwin at the helm, Emma as the indispensable first mate. Emma was the "angel in the house," the ideal Victorian woman. They got along well—when she got morning sickness, he'd get nauseous too—except that she was looser about neatness. (Darwin kept an immaculately clean and ordered study.) In the evenings, she would play piano for him or do needlework in his study, sitting "as quiet as a mouse."

They always had plenty of help—housemaids, butlers, nurses, gardeners. His boys were sent to private tutors, the best prep schools, and then Cambridge. Even though Ras and others were starting to champion equal education for girls, Darwin was old-fashioned. The girls stayed at home and had governesses who taught music, needlework, etiquette, and French, but no science or math.

All his children, however, assisted in his work. Some of their earliest memories were of playing some practical role, as when the family did experiments with thirty different types of peas, dusting bees with flour to see how many pea plants they visited.

Unbeknownst to Darwin, someone else was researching peas at the same time, with astounding results. In Germany, starting in 1856, priest-scientist Gregor Mendel spent seven years studying some 29,000 pea plants and discovering how they produced variations, how genetic traits were passed down through generations. Mendel is now known as the father of modern genetics, and his work supplies the one puzzle piece that Darwin's theory was missing—the mechanism (genes) for passing down inherited traits. But Mendel was laboring in obscurity; his work went unnoticed until after his death some thirty years later.

From peas Darwin turned to pigeons. He threw himself into breeding them, with the children's help, and going to pigeon shows. (Pigeons were considered by the Victorians to be very fashionable birds.)

Darwin also tracked the activity of worms in the soil of Down House gardens. He studied seeds. He analyzed owl poo to see how many seeds could still germinate after being digested. He experimented with seeds soaked in saltwater for many days, proving that they could still germinate and take root . . . which would explain how the seeds of new species traveled from the South American mainland to oceanic islands like the Galápagos.

As the years passed, he was becoming a bit bolder about sharing his new ideas with trusted friends. Some of them tried to persuade Darwin to publish his work soon.

Darwin resisted, consumed with perfectionism: He was "overwhelmed with my riches in facts, and I mean to make my Book as perfect as ever I can."

His friends were right. If Mr. Vestiges's book had trod on some of the same ground as Darwin's theory, Darwin could dismiss it as the work of an amateur, not a man of science. But then in 1858 a true bombshell struck. Darwin received a package from Indonesia. Alfred Russel Wallace was a self-educated naturalist who had loved Darwin's *Voyage of the Beagle.* Fourteen years younger, from the working class, Wallace supported himself by traveling to the jungles of the world and collecting rare natural history specimens that he would later sell. Darwin didn't recall ever meeting Wallace but knew him by reputation as someone working on the same questions as he was. In fact, a year earlier, he had asked if Wallace could please get him some skins from Malaysian poultry.

But there were no chicken skins inside this package. Wallace had written a little essay that set out a species origin theory nearly identical to Darwin's.

Deep in a rainforest somewhere, inspired by "Mr. Vestiges," Wallace had combined ideas from Lyell and Malthus and applied them to the struggle for survival in nature. Though he did not use the exact term "natural selection," Wallace had reached a natural, not divine, explanation for the evolution of species over long periods of time. He'd had a sudden, eureka-type intuition.

Now he was seeking advice. Would Darwin be kind enough, Wallace asked ever so politely, to help him with publication?

Oops.

CHAPTER NINE
The Book That Changed the World

DARWIN'S VERY FIRST reaction was a rare burst of anger. Had he been brooding on his theory for twenty years, only to see his life's work upstaged by someone else?

Yet, always a gentleman, he wanted to do the right thing—give Wallace priority, the important acknowledgment in science that gives someone credit as being the first to make a discovery.

Now Lyell and Hooker, his most loyal friends and men who were at the top of their fields, stepped in. They argued that evolution was simply in the air, finding an explanation for how it happened was only a matter of time, and now time was of the essence. Darwin was wrong, they said, about Victorian society: it was more open-minded than Darwin feared. Science meant progress, new ideas and discoveries. It was urgent for Darwin to establish priority for his evolution theory.

Rather than Darwin handing credit to Wallace on a silver platter, Lyell and Hooker suggested a compromise. They would present *both* men's work to the world's oldest biological society, the Linnean Society of London, named for Swedish botanist Carl Linnaeus, with evidence that Darwin had been working on his theory for years.

Darwin agreed, distracted, haunted by nightmares. At the same time, one of his daughters was seriously ill and his baby son Charles was dying of scarlet fever. He and Emma were staying up nights nursing them.

So, in July 1858, Lyell and Hooker presented Wallace's essay, extracts from Darwin's unpublished work of 1844, and an 1857 letter from Darwin to Asa Gray, an important professor of botany at Harvard, in which he had laid out his theory. Darwin was unable to present his own work. On the very day of the meeting he and his family buried baby Charles.

Oddly enough, the presentation didn't create much of a stir among the thirty eminent men of science at the Linnean Society. Perhaps they didn't understand what a giant shift in thinking the papers represented. Perhaps they were blurry from hearing five other papers, on botany and zoological matters. Neither Wallace nor Darwin was there to question or debate. Their absence made the event less exciting. The president of the society, in one of those famous misjudgments in history, later summed up 1858 as lacking "any of those striking discoveries which at once revolutionize."

The papers were officially published in the society's journal that August. Wallace, like Darwin, was gracious and honorable. When told of Darwin's earlier research and the meeting at the Linnean Society, he accepted co-credit for the theory. Having his name permanently linked to Darwin's was not such a bad thing.

To Darwin's happy surprise, there was no angry response to his paper. Thus, he immersed himself in finishing the book that would change the world: *On the Origin of Species by Means of Natural Selection, or the Preservation of Favored Races in the Struggle for Life.*

He worked furiously, harder than ever before, not at a desk, but writing in his horsehair-stuffed armchair allowed him to shift around to reach books, microscope, snuffbox, or his working table as needed. He wrote for the next thirteen months.

In the middle of the project he did start vomiting again and was forced to take rest breaks at spas, read popular novels of the day, and take up pool playing.

He wanted his book to be as reader-friendly as possible. So it opened with topics that he knew most people would enjoy—dogs and pigeons. (In fact, one of the readers hired by the publisher advised him to stick to these matters, without all that philosophizing afterward.)

He quoted a pigeon breeder describing his breeding timetable, saying he could produce the type of feathers he desired in a pigeon in three years, but it took six years to breed pigeons with a particular head and beak. Crossbreeding was a process of selection Darwin labeled "artificial"—the breeder was in control. But, he went on, the process of selection could also occur by "natural" means, with the environment doing the selecting. The breeder was removed from the equation.

A breeder could improve a species in three to six years, but those changes would be small ones. Imagine the possibilities through the process of natural selection: over *millions* and *billions* of years a flying dinosaur could become a chicken. The theory of natural selection

the possibilities through the process of natural selection: over *millions* and *billions* of years a flying dinosaur
could become a chicken. The theory of natural selection
ran counter to the biblical estimate of the earth's age.
Four thousand years simply wasn't long enough for these
kinds of monumental changes. Living at Down House
had brought home for Darwin how "incomprehensively
vast" past ages had been—he once calculated that it had
taken 300 million years for a nearby valley to form. The
mind can barely grasp such numbers, he admitted.

He explained the ideas about the struggle for existence he'd gleaned from Malthus, applying them to the
plant and animal kingdoms. The idea of a harmonious
universe was an illusion, he said—even the "peaceful"
green fields of England were really a battleground, with
all organisms fighting to survive.

Over many generations, organisms adapt to
their environment. That was key to his theory of
evolution—the notion that all species of living things
change over time through natural selection. He didn't
invent evolution, but he was the first to work out the
mechanism by which it seemed to work. He didn't even
use the word "evolution," but instead "descent with
modification," meaning that more complicated organisms descended from simpler ones. This was the culmi-

nation of all his thoughts since he'd started wondering about the variations among the wildlife he'd encountered in the Galápagos.

Tiny simple organisms were born with mutations, or changes. Some of these enabled the organisms to survive longer and reproduce more. The mutations were passed on via reproduction. So, slowly, over billions of years, as changes accumulated, organisms became more and more complex. Thinking back to the finches on the different islands of the Galápagos, Darwin realized that he had seen evidence of the development of new species. Finches with different beaks were the result of adaptation to a particular food supply. This explained the incredible diversity of life on Earth.

The whole process was random, chancy. This was Darwin's biggest difference from others speaking of evolution, such as his grandfather, who believed in a creator controlling the modification of species, or Lamarck, who thought creatures could will changes in themselves and pass them down. Darwin's natural selection was "blind," even cruel, with no goal except survival and reproductive success.

Darwin had no math equations or decisive experiments to back up his theory. But he gave predictions that could be tested. For example, he thought researchers

would discover "intermediate forms" of organisms connected by common descent, species that some would
come to call "missing links."

He anticipated problems people would find in
his reasoning and addressed them in "Difficulties on
Theory." A bit as he had in his for-and-against marriage list, he enumerated objections and gave answers.
For example, with those intermediate forms of organisms: why don't we see them everywhere? Darwin
asked, "Why is not all nature in confusion instead of
the species being, as we see them, well-defined?" Answer: Because natural selection goes "hand in hand"
with extinction—each new form will tend to make previous "less favored forms" become extinct.

He showed the various ways his theory could be
applied in biology, and asked readers to consider them.
Then he drew to a close by calling his book "one long
argument" linking two ideas: natural selection and
common descent. Creation of animal and plant life did
not happen in six days and then stay the same forever—
higher forms evolved from the lower forms over enormous periods of time. Tantalizingly, he added, "Light
will be thrown on the origin of man and his history."
This was a bit of a tease—the one and only reference
to man in the book. Nor did he make a connection

between man and monkeys. He was waiting to go into depth on this topic in a later book.

Now with priority established, he welcomed the contributions of others: "I look with confidence to the future, to young and rising naturalists, who will be able to view both sides of the question with impartiality."

His last sentence became famous: "There is grandeur in this view of life . . ." he stated; "from so simple a beginning endless forms most beautiful and most wonderful have been and are being evolved."

The strength of the book was his mountain of data from every area of biology known at the time—dozens of examples from nature, from the simplest algae to the most complex flowers, barnacles, primroses, bumblebees, hummingbirds, gooseberries, and, of course beetles. He observed, described, compared, argued, related experiments he had conducted or read about, quoted hundreds of experts he had consulted. Evidence of such scientifically sound labor put the book in a very different league from the efforts of Mr. Vestiges, and the wealth of evidence he offered distinguished it from Wallace's essay.

Also strengthening his credibility was that, unlike Mr. Vestiges, Darwin didn't hide behind a fake name. After all these years, he was finally so confident of his work that he was ready to take complete responsibility.

Most other landmark works of science, such as Newton's *Principia* or Einstein's books on his mindbending theory of relativity, are virtually unreadable for the average person. Darwin's book, however, was an engrossing read. He mastered the art of persuasive writing, not at all arrogant or stuffy. As one of his sons said later, his writing style "revealed his personal sweetness of character to so many who had never seen him." He was the ultimate nice guy, and this likeability helped win over people to his argument.

He had hoped his book would be popular, even if controversial, and was prepared to pay for publication himself. But he did find a publisher fascinated with science who understood that controversy could be good for business.

"I am becoming as weak as a child, miserably unwell and shattered," he wrote during the proofreading process. Emma read it all, pointing out places where she didn't think he was clear enough. She had mellowed, and sometimes they even came close to joking about their religious differences.

At age fifty-one, he published this green volume of 502 pages called, for short, *On the Origin of Species.*

Its main competition for sales that day was Dickens's *A Tale of Two Cities*. All 1,250 copies of Darwin's book sold on the first day, though each copy cost more than a week's pay for a typical working person.

Publication day, November 24, 1859, is considered the birthday of modern biology.

On the Origin of Species has become one of the most influential books ever written. Sending it out into the world, he wrote, "So much for my abominable volume, which has cost me so much labor that I almost hate it."

On publication day, he was a limp noodle, on one of his water cures, trying to get his stomach to settle down.

CHAPTER TEN
The Book That Ate Its Author

$\mathcal{D}$ARWIN SET OUT to devote the rest of his life to promoting the book, not in person—shudder—but indirectly. With sweet letters, he mailed out copies to his eighty best friends, people he knew would talk it up.

By now Darwin had tentacles everywhere, connections with the most influential scientists, in particular four very distinguished cheerleaders who gave loud roars of approval.

Charles Lyell, devoutly religious, began introducing the book in his lectures despite his personal discomfort with some parts of Darwin's theory. He would point out how statements in the book were supported by recent discoveries of Stone Age tools in Northern France. The tools, some 600,000 years old, were found in the same deposits as fossils of extinct animals. This was proof that, as Darwin said, man had existed for much longer than previously thought.

To the well-known English biologist Thomas Huxley, Darwin's theory was so self-evident that he said, "How stupid not to have thought of it before!" What a giant of science was Darwin to connect the dots. Under someone else's name, Huxley wrote an ecstatic review in the *Times*, the journalistic pillar of the British establishment.

Asa Gray, the most important botanist in America by far, succeeded in circulating Darwin's ideas in the American scientific community. Darwin said later, "No one other person understands me so thoroughly as Asa Gray. If ever I doubt what I mean myself, I think I shall ask him!"

Joseph Hooker, his fourth cheerleader, promoted Darwin to the botanists at the Royal Botanic Gardens at Kew, where he was director. The gardens were a government-owned center of research, and new advances in growing tea, sugar, and cotton were crucial to increasing the power of the British Empire. Getting the support of this prominent crowd was a vote of confidence for Darwin.

The book also made a huge splash with the public, which was growing ever more fascinated with science. People went to lectures on electricity, followed the new developments in chemistry. It was a new age of mass media, and Darwin benefited from an amazing increase in the availability of printed materials (at least 150 magazines and newspapers for sale in London), the increase in literacy, and the new leisure time to ponder the big questions. The right book at the right time—the public was ready.

Ras, ever the loyal brother, said, "I really think it is the most interesting book I ever read."

His friend Harriet Martineau added, "We must all be glad that he has set the world on this great new track."

Even Queen Victoria praised one of her daughters for plowing through Mr. Darwin's book.

Alfred Russel Wallace was Darwin's fierce backer, at least for a while. The book "will live as long as the *Principia* of Newton," he wrote. Darwin helped Wallace get a government pension, and they stayed friends, though Wallace drifted away from biology, pulled instead to spiritualism and séances ("rubbish," per Darwin). Wallace also came to believe in an over-riding power that controlled evolution. To this Darwin scrawled a firm, "No!!!"

The Reverend Charles Kingsley, an important writer and prominent Anglican parson, became the first clergyman to state that Darwin's science was perfectly compatible with religion. Kingsley thought you could accept Darwin's ideas and still believe in a God "that created a few original forms capable of self-development into other and needful forms." So it was possible to reconcile belief in a divine power with this theory of life.

But attacks on the book were immediate. The very first review was violently negative, claiming it promot-ed the "men from monkeys" idea, although Darwin had not even mentioned this notion in *Origin*. (It was Mr. Vestiges who had.)

Captain FitzRoy hated it and blamed himself for giving Darwin his start by taking him on the *Beagle*. Darwin's old professor Sedgwick hated it too—parts of his former pupil's work were "utterly false and griev-ously mischievous."

Some called the book blasphemous, actually illegal, for seeming to question God. To some the book was dangerous, threatening the stability of the nation; many simply could not wrap their heads around it.

The debate was heated.

In one of the most famous "battle scenes" in science, Bishop Samuel Wilberforce led an attack on Darwin's theory at Oxford University in 1860. The scene was a crowded meeting of the British Association for the Advancement of Science. "Is it credible that a turnip strives to become a man?" the bishop mocked, grossly misinterpreting the theory. Thomas Huxley argued the case for Darwin, who was happy to be too ill to attend ("I would as soon have died").

Both sides came away from the evening feeling victorious. Wilberforce needled Huxley as to whether he was descended from monkeys on his grandfather's side or his grandmother's side. Huxley snapped back that he would "unhesitatingly" prefer an ape as his ancestor rather than a man such as the bishop who used his intelligence and eloquence "for the mere purpose of introducing ridicule into a grave scientific discussion."

Meanwhile a rowdy audience of several hundred cheered and booed, or sometimes shouted, "Monkey,

monkey!" Some women fainted. FitzRoy showed up, waving his Bible emotionally in the air, yelling, "The Book! The Book!" (Five years later FitzRoy was to commit suicide at age fifty-nine.)

The uproar only made *Origin* of interest to an even wider audience.

Huxley went on to establish himself as "Darwin's bulldog" over the next thirty years. He was the public face, the marketer for evolution, especially in his popular lectures to the working class. In a way he did the dirty work for his friend, who so loathed confrontation.

After the meeting in Oxford, Darwin's book gained much wider acceptance. After 1860 most critics were ministers, attacking the theory on religious grounds. Gradually, the book established itself as a staple scientific text.

In 1863, Henry Walter Bates published a book on the amazing collection of butterflies he had amassed along the Amazon. His discovery of several transitional forms in between different species supplied the first real evidence for Darwin's prediction of missing links.

Darwin's ideas took hold and were applied to totally unrelated areas like business, studies on how we acquire language, and psychology. Sigmund Freud was a huge fan, always calling him "the *great* Darwin." Poets such as Poet Laureate Alfred Tennyson and Matthew Arnold were intrigued, novelist George Eliot was inspired, and in America Henry David Thoreau and Ralph Waldo Emerson appreciated Darwin's explanations of nature's mysteries.

Caricatures of Darwin with the body of an ape or monkey started to appear, some good-humored, some not. He collected them. As if they were beetle specimens, he clipped all reviews (more than two thousand), filing them carefully in scrapbooks, complete with indexes, scrawling testy comments in the margins— "false," "rubbish," "what a quibble." He also wrote some five hundred letters a year in support of his work, begging for feedback.

He never considered *On the Origin of Species* quite finished. He was always making improvements to his theory, strengthening his case, including new facts. The book went through six editions in his lifetime. Not until the fifth edition did he start using "survival of the fittest" to describe his natural selection theory. The phrase, so closely associated with Darwin, was coined in 1864 by philosopher Herbert Spencer, and Wallace had urged Darwin to borrow it.

The book would sell 25,000 copies during his life-time. He had negotiated a very favorable contract for himself, but the pressure drained him. "I am really quite sick of myself," he wrote. A new neighbor encountered this "shy and nervous man" on his daily walk, in black clothes and a cape, wrapped in a gray shawl. He grew frailer, knowing that the controversy he had started would not be settled any time in the near future.

Very true.

CHAPTER ELEVEN
In Need of Soothing

*A*FTER GETTING HIS masterpiece out there, Darwin spent most of the next twenty years soothing his nerves. How so? By embarking on a scientific exploration of exotic plants.

First he became obsessed with tricky plants like sundews and Venus flytraps that snare and digest flies and spiders with their tentacles. He happily tested their reactions with everything he could think of, including his own urine, mucous, and saliva.

Next up was ten solid months focused on the complex beauty of orchids, or rather their love lives, which were amazingly similar to barnacles'. Based on his observations of wild orchids growing in the countryside around Down House, he published *On the Various Contrivances by Which British and Foreign Orchids Are Fertilized by Insects and on the Good Effects of Intercrossing.* This 1862 tome with such a mouthful of a title was not a page-turner or a bestseller, but it persuaded many botanists still on the fence about evolutionary theory. He showed how the "endless diversity of structure" in species of orchids was all for the purpose of fertilization. Orchids had evolved with each part of a flower adapting to allow pollination by flying insects. This was scientific theory, as opposed to the notion that flowers were divinely designed to give humans pleasure and beauty.

He spoke about orchids briefly at the Linnean Society. Alas, this "brought on 23 hours vomiting," with loud retching.

In all he did now, he was looking for further evidence to support his theory. Also research was an acceptable excuse to stay home and avoid the spotlight. He spent six years on his next book, *The Variation of Animals and Plants under Domestication*, collecting evidence about variations in cucumbers, chickens, goldfish, honeybees—evidence that supported statements in *Origin*. This was not a bestseller either—the public craved more about apes.

More and more Darwin was an invalid, spending hours or days vomiting or more accurately, retching, since little came up except acid, which wore away his teeth. Always cold, he kept a fire going year-round in his study, wearing wool underwear under several layers of clothes. His untrimmed beard grew increasingly out of control.

Somehow he managed to keep writing books. Actually he felt worse if he wasn't absorbed in work. Emma and his daughters helped extensively with proofreading and other details. In the evenings he tried to relax playing backgammon with Emma; they kept a running score which at one point was 2,795 (him) to 2,490 (her).

He built an expensive hothouse for peaceful hours observing his plants and conducting meticulous experiments. He was no techie. For the most part he preferred old-fashioned equipment. Science was becoming a profession, shifting from private homes to university labs. One son desperately urged him to get more sophisticated equipment but, like his frugal father before him, Darwin didn't see the point in spending the money, even though by this time he had a great deal of it. Always a compulsive record keeper, he kept financial notebooks for the forty-three years of his marriage, noting every investment, every expense, no matter how tiny.

He was proud of his children and their accomplishments. Most of them went on to have distinguished careers; three of his sons were named Fellows of the Royal Society for their work in science.

In 1864 his "bulldog" Huxley met with Hooker, Spencer, and others to form what became the influential X Club. It was devoted to "science, pure and free, untrammeled by religious dogmas," and it helped Darwin's ideas spread further into British culture. Huxley was later to coin the word "agnostic"—someone who believes it's impossible to know whether God does or does not exist. Darwin applied this label to himself, saying that he really didn't know: things in nature were "so obscure that we stand in awe before the mystery of life." He studied a little about Islam, Hinduism, Buddhism, and other religions, and he saw Christianity as on a par with but not superior to other beliefs. He thought that the concept of God was beyond the mind of man, and also that religion was a very private matter.

Endearingly, he sometimes looked past his own theory when face-to-face with some marvel of nature. Once he picked a flower and questioned how such stunning, intricate beauty could simply be the result of random forces. His visitor joked, "My dear sir, allow me to advise you to read a book called *The Origin of Species.*"

As his health continued its decline, Darwin lay on his sickbed in a room filled with inventive experiments to trace the movements of climbing plants. He would stare at potted plants for hours—did their tendrils go clockwise or counterclockwise? Which plants moved faster?

He also kept working on a sort of sequel to *Origin*, what he called his "Man book." In it he actually stated for the first time the ideas he'd previously been ridiculed for. With *The Descent of Man and Selection in Relation to Sex*, published in 1871, he focused his theories of evolution on humans. Humans, he theorized, were part of the animal kingdom. (Teasingly, he once said his own Emma was "the most interesting specimen in the whole series of vertebrate animals.") He presented evidence for the connection, such as the fact that diseases could be communicated between man and other animals, proving "the close similarity of their tissues and blood."

He noted that from what we know of the development of human fetuses, we could conclude that our prehistoric ancestors, both male and female, were covered in hair, and both had beards. From a mass of evidence like this, he concluded: "We thus learn that man is descended from a hairy quadruped, furnished with a tail and pointed ears, probably arboreal in its habits, and an inhabitant of the Old World."

This was arguably the most controversial sentence ever written in science. He didn't mean that man was descended directly from monkeys, but that both man and monkey were descendants, with modifications, of a common hairy primate ancestor. He had no prehistoric human fossils to work with, but our skeletal resemblance to gorillas and chimpanzees, animals of Africa, allowed him to speculate that this was where humans had first developed. He suspected that someday fossils would be found of an "intermediate form," a creature in between man and his apelike ancestor.

Grouping humans with the rest of the animal world was in no way demeaning to humans, not in Darwin's mind. Underscoring what makes us human (the ability to reason, making tools, self-awareness, language, abstract thought, moral sense, appreciation for beauty), he pointed out simpler forms of the same behaviors in animals. All creatures are connected, all part of the tree of life. Human civilization had tempered the brutal "survival of the fittest" battle—we have the potential to protect life with medicines, caring for the weak and helpless, *not* letting them die.

Descent of Man sold well, not provoking a furor. His work was becoming more and more socially acceptable, much to his relief—"everybody is talking about it without being shocked," he noted. The first children's books on evolution were appearing. Charles Lyell was starting to use the phrase "missing links"— exactly what Darwin had predicted with "intermediate forms" connected by common descent.

The following year, at age sixty-three, he published *The Expression of Emotions in Man and Animals*. Readers were fascinated with his ideas about the similarity of facial expressions among people and animals all over the world. One of the first books to feature printed photographs, this was his biggest bestseller thus far.

His next book, *Insectivorous Plants*, was followed by *The Power of Movement in Plants*, written with his son Francis.

In 1876, he started writing an autobiography. It was not meant for publication, but a grandchild was on the way and he wanted to share his story with future generations of Darwins. He avoided anything too emotional or painful or controversial.

He did worry that his mind was atrophying, becoming "a kind of machine for grinding general laws out of a large collection of facts." But he never lost his childlike sense of wonder about nature, the trait that had started him asking so many questions. One of his sons remembered his gentle touch of a flower—"it was a kind of gratitude to the flower itself, and a personal love for its delicate form and color."

And when his grandson Bernard arrived, he didn't study him scientifically as he'd done with his own children. His simply enjoyed their daily conversations and walks around the garden, timing Bernard's tricycle races up and down the path—just for the joy of being with him.

Thinking about his daughter Annie still made him cry. When the germ theory of infection was finally developed in 1877, he realized how powerful the tiny bacteria were, how much the new research could have helped Annie.

He published his earlier notes on "The Natural History of Babies" as "A Biographical Sketch of an Infant." One of the first articles on child behavior, it led to new research on infant development—what was due to nature, what was because of nurture.

His last book was on worms, which had always mesmerized him. "He has taken to training earthworms," wrote Emma, tolerant as ever. He believed that lowly worms, with their gradual but significant effects on soil, were shortchanged by scientists—they were clearly creatures "which have played so important a part in the history of the world." Now he tested their behavior. Did they react to tobacco fumes, a whistle blowing, vibrations when Emma played piano? Would they eat the tiny triangles and diamonds he cut out of paper? He would observe them outside by moonlight, or creep downstairs to see what they might be up to in his potted plants. He may not have found emotions in them, but they evoked his—affection, amusement, exasperation.

Weirdly enough, *The Formation of Vegetable Mold Through the Action of Worms* turned out to be a blockbuster. A day after publication, his publisher wrote "3,500 *Worms*!!!" Plenty of others found them fascinating, too, and not the least controversial.

Ras was still an important part of his life, a source of gossip and encouragement, a superb uncle to his children. But his beloved brother died in 1881. Darwin called him "the most pleasant and clearest headed man whom I have ever known."

Less than a year later, Charles Darwin died of heart failure. For all his ailments, he lasted until the age of seventy-three. He worked until two days before his death on April 19, 1882. His last words were to his family, assuring Emma, "I am not the least afraid of death."

His plan was to be buried alongside Ras and his daughter Annie in the local churchyard. But the family bowed to pressure from his important friends and supporters.

Darwin was given the most lavish of funerals and buried in Westminster Abbey, close to the great physicist Isaac Newton. England's royalty, leading politicians, scientists, and clergy were all in attendance.

The worm book had been a fitting end to his career—billions of worms, over billions of years, turning over soil, changing the earth, the tiny accumulations of change he loved to think about. Humble, agreeable creatures—nice ones.

CHAPTER TWELVE
Darwin Never Dies

S O MUCH HAS been written about Charles Darwin. Why add another book to the pile?

Because two hundred years after his birth, many people still don't understand his work, and the debate over it still rages.

Darwin's theory of evolution by natural selection opened up an exceptionally rich, yeasty area for further study in biology. As an explanation for biological change, a framework for investigation, Darwin's theory is priceless. As a well-known 1973 essay puts it, "Nothing in biology makes sense except in light of evolution."

But Darwin's reach stretched farther than biology.

His work was a spur to many fields of study in the nineteenth century, leading to waves of progress in psychology, anthropology, medicine, agriculture, and biotechnology, and had an indirect effect on art, literature, and philosophy. It was part of a serious shift in thinking—the universe is not permanent but fluid, changeable. Moreover, all creatures on Earth share connections. He flung open the door to huge areas of ongoing research. Thanks to his painstaking labor, science in general became more established, more of a discipline.

Then, at the turn of the twentieth century, Gregor Mendel's brilliant work in genetics became known and widely accepted. The Austrian scientist had died in obscurity in 1884. It took until the 1930s before scientists realized how much Mendel's work vindicated Darwin's. Passing traits down from one generation to the next— Darwin knew this happened; Mendel showed exactly how it worked.

Combining Mendel with Darwin is known as the "modern synthesis," and it forms the basis of all modern biology and genetics. Scientists consider it the best way of understanding life on Earth, the similarities and differences among living things over time, and what might happen in the future.

Scientific evidence for Darwin's theory mounted

and became overwhelming. Marie Curie's discovery of radioactivity in the 1890s led to carbon dating, which confirmed that the earth was much older than those before Darwin had believed. Biblical scholars had established the Creation at 4004 B.C. Today the latest estimate of our planet's age is about 4.5 billion years old.

Transitional fossils—the "intermediate forms" he predicted—continue to be found. One of the major finds was Lucy, the fossilized skeleton of a creature less than four feet tall, with some ape traits and some humanlike traits, discovered in Ethiopia in 1974. Lucy (named after the Beatles' song "Lucy in the Sky with Diamonds") is estimated to be 3.2 million years old.

In 2006 University of Chicago researchers discovered the tiktaalik, a transitional species of fish. Estimated to be 375 million years old, with fins that functioned like legs, it was a transition between fish and four-legged animals.

The most hardened resistance to Darwin's theory is in the United States, where scientific literacy lags behind that of other industrialized nations. A significant percentage of Americans do not accept the theory of evolution and think that all the supporting evidence for it has been somehow faked or staged.

In the United States the Constitution provides a separation of church and state, meaning the government does not support any particular religion. Public schools, funded by the government, therefore, do not teach religion. Yet, through court cases, religious groups have long tried to keep Darwin out of the classroom on the basis that his theory contradicts the Bible's story of Creation.

The most famous court case involving evolution was the "Monkey Trial" of 1925.

John Scopes, who taught biology in Tennessee, discussed evolution with his students, in violation of the new state law that made it illegal to teach anything that contradicted the biblical story of Creation.

Scopes was arrested, and at his trial, lawyers on both sides argued passionately for ten days. The entire nation was spellbound. Scopes was found guilty, which led other states to ban the teaching of evolution.

Later on, Scopes's conviction was overturned on a technicality, and every subsequent court case since then involving the teaching of evolution has resulted in a verdict supporting the separation of church and state.

Yet in the last fifty years, in the United States creationism (a word coined in 1868 to describe opposition to Darwin) has become more popular than ever, its proponents claiming scientific evidence in support of the biblical version of Creation. Intelligent Design, a concept introduced in 1989, is a variation on creationism stating that an intelligent being—never specifically called God—is the controlling force behind life on Earth. Creationists argue that their theory of the beginning of life should be included in textbooks alongside evolution.

It is important to note that many scientists with strong religious beliefs see no conflict between science and their faith in God. These are just two different ways of understanding the world and don't have to cancel each other out. In September 2008, the Church of England, in advance of the two hundredth anniversary of Darwin's birth, issued a belated apology to Darwin "for misunderstanding you and, by getting our first reaction wrong, encouraging others to misunderstand you still."

So much of cutting-edge science is based on Darwin. Since evolution is ongoing and unpredictable, we need to learn about it to find ways to solve problems— what we can do to prevent animals from becoming extinct and bacteria becoming resistant to antibiotics, and to help us to identify and treat new viruses like the one that causes swine flu.

Today, to some extent, we can control things in nature that would have killed us in the past—we have vaccines for smallpox, for example. We no longer have to be the fastest or strongest in order to survive, as long as we have access to proper medicine. But will advances in health lead to even more severe overpopulation? What climate changes are in store for us and how will we adapt? In the future, will we genetically engineer ourselves?

So many questions, so many intriguing topics to explore and debate. Were he still here, Darwin would be astonished, but he'd adapt—and he'd be furiously taking notes.

SOURCES

(*especially for young readers)

BOOKS

Berra, Tim M. *Charles Darwin: The Concise Story of an Extraordinary Man*. Baltimore: Johns Hopkins University Press, 2009.

Browne, Janet. *Charles Darwin, Volume 1: Voyaging*. New York: Knopf, 1995.

Browne, Janet. *Charles Darwin, Volume 2: The Power of Place*. New York: Knopf, 2002.

Browne, Janet. *Darwin's Origin of Species: A Biography*. New York: Atlantic Monthly Press, 2006.

Darwin, Charles. *On the Origin of Species: The Illustrated Edition*, edited by David Quammen. New York: Sterling, 2008.

*Heiligman, Deborah. *Charles and Emma: The Darwins' Leap of Faith*. New York: Holt, 2009.

*Jenkins, Steve. *Life on Earth: The Story of Evolution*. Boston: Houghton Mifflin, 2002.

Keynes, Randal. *Darwin, His Daughter, and Human Evolution*. New York: Riverhead Books, 2002.

*Lasky, Kathryn. *One Beetle Too Many: The Extraordinary Adventures of Charles Darwin*. Somerville, Mass.: Candlewick, 2009.

*Lawson, Kristan. *Darwin and Evolution for Kids: His Life and Ideas with 21 Activities*. Chicago: Chicago Review Press, 2003.

Milner, Richard. *Darwin's Universe: Evolution from A to Z*. Berkeley: University of California Press, 2009.

*Patent, Dorothy Hinshaw. *Charles Darwin: The Life of a Revolutionary Thinker*. New York: Holiday House, 2001.

Quammen, David. *The Reluctant Mr. Darwin: An Intimate Portrait of Charles Darwin and the Making of His Theory of Evolution*. New York: Norton, 2006.

*Sis, Peter, *The Tree of Life: A Book Depicting the Life of Charles Darwin, Naturalist, Geologist, and Thinker*. New York: Farrar Straus, 2003.

*Strathern, Paul. *Darwin and Evolution*. London: Arrow Books, 1998.

WEB SITES

American Museum of Natural History, Darwin: http://www.amnh.org/exhibitions/darwin/

CARTA, The Center for Academic Research and Training in Anthropogeny: http://carta.anthropogeny.org/

The Complete Works of Charles Darwin Online:
http://darwin-online.org.uk

International Darwin Day Foundation, Celebrating Darwin,
Science and Humanity:
http://www.darwinday.org/darwin

Linnean Society of London:
http://www.linnean.org/

National Center for Science Education: Defending the Teaching of
Evolution in Public Schools: http://ncse.com

National Science Teachers Association, Evolution Resources:
http://www.nsta.org/publications/evolution.aspx?lid=tnav

The Natural History Museum, London, Darwin 200:
www.darwin200.org

PBS, Evolution, Darwin's Dangerous Idea:
http://www.pbs.org/wgbh/evolution/darwin/index.html

INDEX

Note: Page numbers in *italics* indicate illustrations.

JUNIATA COLLEGE

2820 9100 111 677 1

WITHDRAWN
JUNIATA COLLEGE LIBRARY

CURRICULUM LIBRARY